The New Arcana

To Kyle —
with many
best wishes
for an inspired 2013,

[signature]

12/16/12

The New Arcana

John Amen
and
Daniel Y. Harris

www.nyqbooks.org

NYQ Books™ is an imprint of the The New York Quarterly Foundation, Inc.

The New York Quarterly Foundation, Inc.
P.O. Box 2015
Old Chelsea Station
New York, NY 10013

www.nyqbooks.org

First Edition

Set in Minion Pro and Myriad Light Pro

Layout and Design: Mary Powers | marypowers.com
Production Expertise: Keith Koger | kogercreative.com

Cover Art: "The New Arcana" – Collage on Board
Copyright © 2012 Mary Powers

Author photo John Amen: Thia Chempanise
Author photo Daniel Y. Harris: Britannia Weatherby

Library of Congress Control Number: 2012945157

ISBN: 978-1-935520-59-7

The New Arcana

SECTION ONE

Dramatis Personae

Jughead Jones
Sadie Shorthand
I or (later) I and I
Austin L. Halford
Enrico the Insouciant
Yolanda the Crone
Albert the Bore
Jacqueline the Mum
EidenberryWhatever
We/Us

I.

"Our Father who art," began Jughead Jones, "quotidian be thy name." He paused, smirked.
"Oh, I suppose it's up to me," Sadie Shorthand blurted, "to dispel *le moment gauche de silence*?"
"I see, another Cartesian dilettante," Jughead muttered, winking at Sadie.
"Who I am essentially is always three steps ahead of who I am incidentally," Sadie replied. "Even
  you, Mr. Don Juan, are an illusion."
"Touché," conceded Jughead and tucked a $20 bill into Sadie's g-string.

A hot wind whips across the eternal landscape;
archaic symbols are sold at auction north of Disneyland
to diehard antique-mongers and melancholy pedants.

> "Dad, what you call your life is just an epistemological construct."
> (Jughead Jones on his tenth birthday)

Flame, clangor, holy superstition of cause and effect.
La religion de séquentialité!

Letters and words clipped from magazines.
The many faces that represent us.

Then, a flipped coin fell from the blue sky like an afterthought.
Will you stick around to hear the details—how it landed—
as they are cast and analyzed by the aging excommunicants?

> Neither success nor failure shall distract us.

At night, I sing ditties in the dark to keep the hunger at bay:
"If bodied, ovum in the seminal green
                    of the divisor, stirred
            to cling and defile,
                quickens its quotient
to evil,
and then evil is sublimed."

The arbiter within lowers his gavel. Ah, let us
snore, snore sweetly in this velvet box of correlatives,
heads propped on a hymnal, calculators in hand.

> "Mathematics is a thousand ladders to nowhere.
> Theology is a newborn sibyl cooing in the darkness."

(comments made by Sadie Shorthand
during her school trip to France when she was sixteen)

"Have any of you coprophiliacs seen Sadie?" Jughead yells through a bullhorn, glowering in the doorway of The Office Club, the strobe light and jukebox wail triggering his epilepsy.

"I think she went to see her astrologer," mumbles a fat man with a black beard. His ectomorphic buddy, bald and goateed, gives him a high-five.

Jughead yanks his resentment pad from his back pocket, does a quick and shaky sketch of the fat man, and marches back into the rain, twitching.

"To be God—now that's a strange karma."
(Sadie Shorthand's quote for her senior yearbook)

II.

I've grown weary
  of my residual self, for whom change
   is a game of mercy with a suspicious stranger.
La vérité en peinture—clamped, sifted, raked, rotted
  down to inherited imagery
  through which I am again deceived.
Wait, not mercy after all,
   but a clashing of fists—*mea culpa*.

"...the 1990s and early 2000s were characterized chiefly by a conservative academic trend which served to marginalize most non-linear techniques, including what came to be known as the neo-Dadaistic 'pre-sabotages' of the 'untenured six.' The release of Sadie Shorthand's *The Crazy Tape*, however, quickly and fundamentally impacted the literary landscape, tipping the scales, admittedly for only a brief time, towards a refreshingly liberal and undeniably expansive aesthetic." (Austin L. Halford, "1985-2010: The Dark Age and Renaissance of Literary Insurgence," first published in *Lexical Fortuities*, Issue 22)

On Monday evening, steering home, I saw a body on a stretcher,
  the mangled car,
   ambulance, gawking drivers,
 autumn leaves falling on the red highway.

"This is my lexical face

pockmarked after a brief stint in academia,
　　　airbrushed post production:

ovate, dyed, darkened
　　　　　　by a chemical wince,

I am, alas, a mummy unwrapped
　　　　　　in time for the faux exhibit."
("Destiny 4" from *The Crazy Tape* by Sadie Shorthand)

Over milk, hypodermic restlessness, and mango sherbet, Sadie and Jughead discuss their fluttering day:
"Some people," Sadie insists, "effaced like nail files, lost in a tangled garden behind a mansion with no street address, simply aren't rebellious."
"Has it occurred to you," Jughead counters, "that when you angle your face towards the sunset, simultaneously bending your index finger in that idiosyncratic way—that when you do all that, you kind of look like Cicero?"
"Bull jazz," exclaims Sadie. "It sounds to me like you think a mammoth wave is cresting over my thwarted intentions."
Jughead begins to retort, thinks better of it, plunges his hypodermic restlessness into the foundering light.

"I'm at my best when I think of myself mathematically." (Jughead)
"I'm at my worst when I think of myself theologically." (Sadie)

Infatuation glows like a right angle—
beware the bare, eroded slope of Eros.
Lovers: exquisite coordinates in nova.

III.

Words, words, words are illusions despite
rigors of coherence, attention to subjective/objective alignments,
a contraction towards metaphoric compromises:
                    the hunt
            for assistants and protégés has begun.
It will be our mission to master
this legerdemain. Nonreader beware!

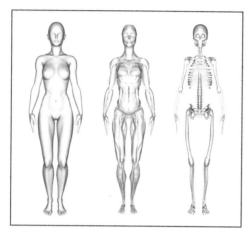

My ennui shall be my tabernacle,
            temple, Delphi.
It shall lead me through rapacious waters,
past sirens and reefs, deliver me
            safe to Ithaca.

"I can't believe how superstitious people are," Sadie
exclaims over puddles of grease and ketchup, perfect
posture in the broken vinyl booth of the all-night
diner, her right eyebrow arched like an A-frame.
"Take Enrico and Yolanda—you know, the cutesy ones,"
she adds, licking her fingers—"their baby had a…
mishap at the World Conference. They're blaming it
on some mathematical inconsistency. I didn't know
this, but apparently God deplores certain numbers."

A stuffed parrot in the bedroom—the virgin bride
(un)shafted, typing up her will on her wedding night.
How immoderate; well, incongruous; well, inconsequential.
Who's the predator *now*?

Have you considered
trying to distinguish the facts from your interpretations?

In Visual Appendix L-3B12, it is surmised by the attendant
on night duty, who customarily wears vintage clothing,
cheap knock-off cologne, and a nuclear earring,
that a glazing of the eyes has much imagistic merit.

"A black house
scrubbed white and fenced;
in the basement, my father, a bronze idol
embalming my mother, a stick figure.
I take a nap on the butcher's block."
(from Sadie Shorthand's *I am a chameleon: dream journal 3*)

From *Galveston Genealogies, 1952*:
"…there is no doubt that Wilbury Galveston was a man
of myriad fetishes; he often showed up at parties dressed
in diapers, clenching between his teeth a rubber pacifier,
begging various women to 'mother' him."

From *Profiles in Aberrancy, 1995*:
"In 1986, during the inaugural World Adult Baby Confer-
ence, Jacques Lyddle-Perierre was awarded the first an-
nual Galveston Prize, which included a year's worth of
milk to be pumped daily from the breasts of a
Hungarian wet nurse."

Jughead Jones fuming in the coffee shop
over blueberry muffins and espresso.
Staring into the rain, he squints his bloodshot eyes.
"Fuck, that's Sadie," he fumes under his breath,
mistaking the silk-flower girl for his Isis/Elizabeth Browning/
iambic Jezebel—and the nerve,
sauntering hand in hand with the doe-eyed cashier
from the Lincoln Avenue Diaper Depot.

Sabbath blabbath.

IV.

Oh, my skeptical colleagues, drawn into this labyrinth,
each twist and turn of which promises,
        I promise, an exit pure and fleeting,
      thank you for setting aside
your theses and theorems:
      our incidental differences
        are of minor concern.

> "She is a virus hellbent on destroying itself.
> He is a panacea hellbent on being needed."
> ("The Lovers" from *The Crazy Tape* by Sadie Shorthand)

"Maybe some suckers," Jughead texts in code. "No, milk, that's what we really need. You know anyone?" He adds a colon-parentheses smiley face, sends the message.
"White galaxy. Remember the cutesy girl?" Sadie texts back. "Maybe her. Do you think we're being watched?"
"Negative," Jughead replies. "I still look good on paper."
"Hmm," responds Sadie, "are you sure you're not just misanthropic?"
Jughead snaps his phone shut. Even the most oblique reference to his prior fiscal failures continues to trigger shame and arousal, the old *coma barbelé*.

For days now, wind and rain,
snakes and moss hanging from the cypress trees
like theological or mathematical proofs.
Milky, formica mornings. Nights darker than newsprint.
Are we about to face some great
and irreversible checkmate?

"*And* is an illusion."
(Sadie Shorthand)

> "The man pulled one of those antique musket-
> pistols from his tuxedo pocket, pointed it, and fired.
> Then everything turned red."
> (witness testimony at the trial of Jughead Jones)

"What the ego can't sweep away,
it simply coats with thought-sugar."
(Enrico the Insouciant)

"The dove and the styrofoam.
A strange pattering of feet
on the hardwood floor.
In other words, I plead the fifth."
(testimony of Albert the Bore at the trial of Jughead Jones)

Oh, my disingenuous censors, gavels in the margins
        of your vitriolic notes—
I'm unconvinced that you critique well—I am not
        disdaining the protocol
                of your habitual cannibalism,
                        but please analyze
your own prejudice,
        consume less of our kind.

"You really need to figure out what's next for you, Sadie.
Math, theology, whatever. Why don't you put out a book?" (Jughead)
"Well, Jug, the truth is, you're my *first* book.
I've been editing you since we met." (Sadie)

V.

"Stars and banners of the new politics," Jughead
　　says aloud, alone in his Corolla, slightly
　　　　manic at midnight on a back road,
　　twiddling the long, brown curls
　　　　　of his rented wig.

"Am I sanctified yet?"
(from the (attempted) suicide note of Yolanda the Crone)

Alas, I am being bombarded by wings, black embers,
velcro, and coupons, Sadie thinks, removing her 4-inch
heels, hanging the riding crop on the smoke-yellow wall.
She can still hear the fraternity boys whooping in the bar,
she of the silver, gleaming pole. She wants to buy a
multi-slice CT scanner, some baklava, an HD television.
If honest, she'd like to teach kindergarten in the Midwest.

Visit our storefront and reference the various
breakdowns with which we contend on a moment-to-
moment basis. Discount Code BL9IU76.
We have been widely recognized by leading media
outlets and endorsed by the National Coalition for the
Advancement of Secular Aesthetics. Some even
associate us with the AVATAR ITSELF.

Too late, between crumbs of Cartesian hypochondria,
　　　　saturated fat of dictum, logic, syllogism,
for Enrico the Insouciant to turn the other cheek,
　　　　not that it's in his nature, brainstorming
　　　　　　behind his George Foreman grill,
　　his Elia Kazan films, his midnight
　　emails to Yolanda the Crone, the way he
flagrantly covets his neighbors' London Broil,
keying their antique Ferrari, sloshing paint
　　　　　on their chemical lawn, overturning
the cardboard pelican announcing the safe arrival
　　　　　　of their second daughter.

"I shall undo myself,"
Sadie mumbles in her cubistic sleep,
her Beatific Mama suit glowing at the foot of the bed.

In the salon next to Mail Boxes Etc., Albert the Bore
gets a Faustian trim to ease his anxiety, his fear of becoming
"a lie incarnate." His posse settles in with hypotheses
and periodicals—sprawling, propping, guffawing, picking
at notorious scabs with penknives and jagged verbs.
"I can delay the inevitable with mandates," says Albert to himself.
"I mean, I can regulate my lacteal need with mantras."
"I wish," says Albert to Yolanda, "despite my rolodex
of impeccable theories, that I understood myself better."
"So much I do indeed control," says Albert to Enrico,
"and then again, so much I am controlled by."
"I am unrecognized—I mean, I feel unrecognized—
yet I make so many heads turn," says Yolanda to Enrico.
"Your pivotal breakthrough," says Enrico to Albert,
"what you have been seeking and avoiding, is just up ahead."
"Damn it, man," says Albert to Enrico, "that nipple
was being reserved for Yolanda, our Sister Climacterica."

"Mommy is everywhere."
(last words of Albert the Bore,
winner of the 2006 Galveston Prize)

"Corduroy and corollaries of a dated diatribe," Sadie
scrawls on her palm, alone in her kitchen, hyperglycemic,
3am with the neon Sodom still shrieking in her ears.
I should dye my hair pistachio, she thinks and giggles,
now strapped and tapping with her quirky index finger
the restless hypo.
Outside her window,
under the dripping eave, Jughead watches,
sketching in his resentment pad.

VI.

"Sadie, it's me,"
repeats Yolanda the Crone, standing in the doorway
of Sadie's place,
waiting, waiting for a reply, then
sauntering towards Sadie's bulging fridge with
Enrico
the Insouciant
freshly tattooed
on her arm.

"Yolanda's neologism," Enrico had quipped
earlier that night at the get-to-know-you, surrounded
by bankers garbed in pink bonnets
and gnawing on pacifiers,
"is antithetical *modus ponens*, if indeed f is a function
of type $P \rightarrow Q$, and x is of type P,
and $f(x)$ is of type Q,
where Q = quagmire or surrogate
for breaking every bone
without pulling the cord."
The room had erupted in laughter: the same joke he told
at the 2004 World Adult Baby Conference.

$$2\text{fortification} + \text{recidivism} = \text{autumn} - 6\text{avalanche}$$

gentrify, gentrify, gentrify.

Albert the Bore,
not amused, his jealousy swarming like a furnace,
had turned to a prodigious woman (the substitute Dark Mother),
complained of Enrico's banality.
"*His* neologisms only refer to *her* private syntax,
and that pidgin Hebrew—you know what I'm saying?—
it just lulls me into a state of absolute catatonia.
I had a friend named Jughead once,
but he was no inquisitor. *He* worked for the phone company.
Line installation and repair was *his* work."

"Albert," Enrico exclaimed, spotting his cohort in crime
by the mango mush. "I see you're still getting

your money's worth. Or should I say girth?"
He got a few laughs, a scowl from Albert.
"By the way," Enrico had continued, "just so you're clear,
                    Yolanda is part Peruvian
            and part Mexican, not Guatemalan,
    and certainly not Norwegian."
                    "OK, Enrico," Albert snapped,
"I guess you don't even remember Jughead Jones?"
"Oh, *I* certainly do," said Yolanda, skipping across the room
            with a green smoothie in a champagne glass.
        "He once read Alexis de Tocqueville to me
            while I chomped on a corndog."
Enrico buried his thumb in the mango mush,
        pretending it was Albert's right eye, and pushed.

                                The night is raw color streaking
                            through my guts like a deranged elephant.

"To Jughead Jones," Enrico said mockingly, causing group discomfort.
"To corndogs," Yolanda added, relaxing jaws and shoulders.
"To ev- ev- evolution," the substitute Dark Mother stuttered, "and ev- ev- everything that gets
left be- be- behind."

Yolanda drinks two glasses of kefir in the milk-white kitchen,
        fixes a tofu sandwich, hypo dessert;
            cleaning up, leaves no trace.
"Have milk, Sadie. Don't be bitter," she texts.
She surveys the place, strolls out, leaves
                the front door wide open behind her.

VII.

Jacqueline the Mum (Austin L. Halford's cousin
    twice removed) need help growing old,
        then a spill on the stair and now she in
    assisted
    living.

"God, what this come down to," she say.
    "My body like some old timepiece
        being taken apart by a hack horologist."

            "Sadie Shorthand is like a demiurge in a postmodern
            Genesis.... Her debut, *The Crazy Tape*, may very well be
            her generation's literary Big Bang." (Austin L. Halford,
            Poetry Engine, Issue 32)

"I ain't garnered a acre in a coupla' year,
    but I better than a upcomer engine any goddamn day,"
        mutter Jacqueline the Mum's neighbor,
Eidenberry Whatever, pretending to push a plow
        down the retirement home corridor.

General Inventory of Items in Eidenberry Whatever's Room:
*Pants, shirts, socks, shoes, etc.
*Various books, including *The Crazy Tape*,
  poetry collection by granddaughter-in-law,
  Sadie Shorthand
*three stacks of magazines, some pornographic
*HD television
*clock radio
*poster of and signed by grandson, Jughead Jones
*Christmas card signed by Albert the Bore
*empty refrigerator
*five large Ziploc bags
  filled with various condiments
*package of adult diapers

"He sure enough was one of the good 'uns,"
    say Jacqueline the Mum
at Eidenberry's April funeral. "I wish I'da met him
        when our parts was still workin'."

"Rope the Critter" was written and performed by Jacqueline the Mum and her band, Angus Hay. The song reached #2 on various music charts and was awarded the 1953 Perkins Prize for the year's best single.

"There is no wager that can keep me
  from my mannequin sky,
  where I relish a codependent clairvoyance
  with a Grim Reaper
  תְּמַה דְּאֶלַם parachute
  ("What Things Become" from *The Crazy Tape* by Sadie Shorthand)

Jacqueline the Mum just prior to
receiving her 1953 Perkins Prize

Sadie and Jughead
at the funeral restless,
strap and hypo tap in
Eidenberry's bathroom.
"Smell," say Jug,
  "of old, old man. Hey, Sadie,"
    he adds, gesturing at some items
      crammed into a bulging box,
        "is that a package of diapers?"

VIII.

Enrico the Insouciant, Yolanda the Crone,
Jughead Jones, and Sadie Shorthand,
known in the Adult Baby chatrooms
as Mr. Lapidary, Ms. Sapphire, Mr. Saltpeter, and Madame Sequential,
were banned from the university's Conference on the Confluence
of Ulcerative Colitis and Libidinal Anomalies,
the restraining order filed at 4:59pm on a Friday.
Seismic activity preempted decorum. When the diaper
splattered against the brick wall littered with ivy,
and a feral dog with hip dysplasia began barking wildly,
a semaphore triggered a tocsin. "Rook to Queen's Pond,"
said Madame Sequential before her sudden regression.
"A pogo stick?" shrieked Mr. Saltpeter.
"I expected a pacifier." The screen went blank.

Backgammon anyone?
I and I is the legacy of cotton and Confederacy,
violence the topsoil of my hankering.
Every scene need a narcissist posing as a benign farmer,
know what I mean?
Someone should release us rural sons
    to our own inner crops,
despite how it nudge out the previous generation:
we young 'uns, we too knows all about debt and fallow fields.

syncopation - regret = nationalism
amnesia + arrogance = capitalism

"What they can't take from you,
 you end up giving them."
 (Sadie Shorthand to a stranger at Eidenberry Whatever's funeral)

"Antiferromagnetism
 with Kagome lattice,

its spun glass: geophysics
of war paint,

chromium alloy to the dead
redux—

the tilting head, chalk red."
("Rectitude" from *The Crazy Tape* by Sadie Shorthand)

> "[Sadie] was the best student I ever had. In less than a year, she mastered the techniques I was offering. Then she proceeded to forge her own new directions, both maximizing and utterly transcending my influence." (Albert the Bore, "Eulogy for Sadie Shorthand," first published in *Poetic Karma*, Issue 11)

Please, blame me, if you wish, for this obvious inversion,
            this *détour sacré* into rooms
        usually closed during the regular weekday tour.
            Pick my scarab-looking scars.
        Drain the fluids of my soggy spirit.
Lance the boils of my recondite, pusillanimous personality
with references to your family Bible, the one wedged between
            the phonebook and the 1977 almanac.
I and I am the barbequed, native son of Nowhere and Failed Objectivism.
I and I was born thirteen miles due East of Elsewhere.
    When you find me by way of radiation-enhanced GPS,
        capture me and cut my body
            into tiny pieces, watch me reconstitute
and blend in like weeds.
            I and I am a thousand no ones,
        a player, trickster, master of blather.

IX.

"Yolanda," whispers Albert,
    "that Algerian stand-in was like a commandant,
ordering me to '*prendre un sucer et se déplacer sur.*'
'But where's Mama?' I kept asking.
        '*Allé,*' she said. '*Je suis votre mère maintenant.*'"

Enrico appears from the adjoining room,
        stethoscope in hand, flipping through
      pages of an old calendar. "Look," he says, pointing
at illegible scrawls in the block of May 3,
    "that's when we founded this happy little quintet.
Albert, you mooch, you drank more than your share, again."

We are speaking here of contingent
or concomitant psychic structures.
These formations are as readily
observed as is the concentric
relation of a quark and an atom.

Oh, my mystical converts,
Sadie, spirit of Sadie, she's now everything everywhere,
a microcosmic reflection of the macrocosmic Wet Nurse.
Dear, dear Sadie. Lunar Sadie. Solar Sadie. Are we not
grateful for the milk of our forgetting?—pan-Sadie!

More importantly, complementary data, demonstrating
the divisive and incidental nature of such formations, can
be utilized as an effective counter argument against

avid proponents of universal notions of causality,
gatekeepers for the objectification of conscious
and/or unconscious collective mandates.

"Here's to some serious revolutionary shit," Jughead slurs,
     throwing back his seventh shot,
belching his hypo frustration into the hovering smoke
    of The Office Club,
sliding his index fingers through front belt loops,
      incendiary naive as a drunk ideologue be.

Albert, of course, has a crush on Yolanda,
  her eyes floating in her palms,
    but his timid way tamped down hard,
his affection cocooned.
   Yolanda counts regrets on her teeth and tongue,
recalls Jug and Sadie confabbing in the milk-white kitchen,
     pacifiers and Lego kits
strewn about the floor, bills unpaid.
Quips about mathematics and theology.
   Secret society.
Double lives. Triple lives.
   Until the milk got too thick. Sour.
"Jealousy," she announces to no one in particular.

       Albert stares at the floor
as Enrico fidgets with his stethoscope. "Life's a crossword,"
   Yolanda adds, crossing her fishnet legs,
     "and all of the clues are red herrings."

Jug, he had a gun.

X.

"…when I encountered the 'diffusion and sabotage' technique as it was being taught by Albert the Bore and seminally applied by Sadie Shorthand amongst others, I was immediately impressed by what was being produced in terms of scope and sublimity. I'm proud to say that I was probably one of the chief proponents of what turned out to be a vital, albeit short-lived, literary movement. I consider so much of what was produced during those few years to be almost celestially inspired, quasi-transmissions of The Source itself…it's uncanny that many of those prodigies and wunderkinds died prematurely, unexpectedly, and/or tragically." (Austin L. Halford, "1985-2010: The Dark Age and Renaissance of Literary Insurgence," first published in *Lexical Fortuities*, Issue 22)

"Anticoagulant dynamism
with Kafkaesque lagniappe:

a worn margin: geocentric
with anthrocentric reference,

world hybrid to the jubilant
canon—

what a leaning tower, gravestone bare."
("Ending" from *The Crazy Tape* by Sadie Shorthand)

"Before love claimed me,
I knew God as the torturer knows his victim;
I mean, in the Pentecostal sense."
(comment made by Jughead Jones
after his conviction of first-degree murder)

"Shall we carry on, then?" asks Enrico,
dish detergent in hand. Yolanda dims,
          her nipples erect
beneath her burlap maternity dress.
          Albert smashes his reading glasses on his thigh,
hurls a signed first edition of *The Crazy Tape*
          out the kitchen window into the boxwood hedge.
                    "You can break
everything in your life," Sadie once said,
"but then you have to take the pieces with you."

search + pyre = attitude – frisson

"Tonight," says Albert, his eyes narrowing,
        "we should draw straws to see who sleeps in the crib."
"And to see who burps whom," exclaims Enrico.
            "And who changes the diapers," ripostes Albert.
        "Actually, count me out,
I'm getting a place with Jacqueline," says Yolanda,
        hurling a breast pump onto the floor. "What was it
that French prima donna said?" she adds. "Oh yeah,
                        'let them drink fucking formula!'"

Then: "I can't believe I just broke my glasses,"
Albert moans. "This doesn't bode well for my phonetics lesson."
"The place is an absolute mess," agrees Enrico. "I suppose
        we'll need to run another ad."
        The empty space where Sadie would have been.

Autopsy of Jughead Jones

SECTION TWO

Dramatis Personae

Constance Carbuncle
Justin Nurm
Dr. Yistrum Lee
Lead Advocate Hortense
I
Judge
Bus Driver
Don the Commuter
Freddie Brill or Sir Adrian the Fop-Murderer
Thaddeus Felino

I.

Constance Carbuncle
waved goodbye
to a few more neurons:
warrior cells and regenerative dendrites
were insufficient to counter her family's wacked legacy.

APPLAUD NOW!

for the barbarians
forming evil legions in her noggin,
darkness expanding,
hillocks like capitulated forts,
mimetic hubs razed by the madness.

"Constance is polysynesthetic," exclaimed Justin Nurm.
"Not to mention logorrheic and auto-allergic,"
diagnosed Dr. Yistrum Lee. "Well, give her
a fucking silence pill. You know, put
her Idea Box to sleep, man," responded Justin.
"Would that really contain her, though?"
pondered Lee. "I mean,
even in catatonia she brandishes that patented Kali complex."
Justin unwrapped his soy sandwich,
popped his knuckles, sighed loudly.

Before her first lobal earthquake, Constance
was dubbed a galactic prodigy, blessed
with four-dimensional visions, a truly acrobatic intellect,
amygdalae pulsing
with the electricity of a two hundred
and eighteen point intelligence quotient.
Fifty to one hundred million simultaneous sparks
stoked her wit, manifesting pure cogito. Her mind
had throbbed like a riptide of molten rock.
Once, prior to her legendary bleeding from the eyes,
she sent improvised tropes soaring weightless
from scaffolds of unbridled imagination,
yoking no less than fourteen deeply disparate metaphors
gilded in sidereal dust:
the perfect marriage of meaning and meaning-making.

Her second-grade art teacher once referred to Constance as "a lacquered torch burning with inexhaustible natural resources, a dragon spitting uncompromised light into the chiaroscuro of a world snoring on duty."

The Dean of Lamboud's Department of Psychology was quoted as saying, "Ah, Constance, she is a rosewood altar upon which rests each of the sacred suburban symbols—crosses, pliers, communion wafers, recording equipment, Tibetan singing bowls, cut and perfectly arranged hydrangeas. In my mind, she displays at least four distinct and paradoxical personalities: the pigtailed cheerleader, the Goth poetess, the street harlot, and, yes, the archetypally bedridden octogenarian."

"Astrological misinterpretations, egregious disloyalty, and psychiatric malfeasance contributed to Constance Carbuncle's collapse as much as if not more than Ms. Carbuncle's obsessive belief in original sin and irrevocable familial karma," reflected Lead Advocate Hortense to a local tabloid writer immediately following Constance Carbuncle's competency hearing.

Famous portrait painter Albay Thompson, for whom Constance once posed, wrote in his memoirs: "Constance's eyebrows were like the eaves of a floating palace, perches for disenfranchised griffins. Incubi and succubi, no doubt, slept occasionally in the faint and premature crow's feet abutting her eyes. I am sure that Beelzebub referred to her furrowed brow as his private think tank."

The archbishop of Hilton, NY, once trapped with Constance in a malfunctioning elevator, later said, "It was as if her skull was a helium balloon rising by corpus flame blasts through the atmosphere. She kept declaring, 'I'm a sooty splashdown occurring invariably at prime time, exploited ceaselessly by a ravenous paparazzi.' I'm just glad we were freed prior to the subsequent combustion."

"Corrupt police, trash-trollers striking for sick pay, the Chamber of Commerce choosing to penalize the homeless—on and on—all this contributed to creating a certain cultural backdrop or collective existential context; and, in my opinion, definitely exacerbated Constance's preexistent fragility," added Justin Nurm, who once flew into a rage when a hotdog vendor neglected to offer him mustard for

his salty pretzel, instead tossing
three yellowish packets of pepper
in his general direction.

Truth: the forehead of Constance, tightly sewn with blessed catgut following the surgery, had once beamed with exemplary, glossy, unwrinkled derma.

Truth: her ogle, known to consistently penetrate encrypted antimatter, inspired the popular iconography of numerous rock stars, agoraphobics, fashionistas, and wannabe romantics.

"Well, she was standing there
lecturing a pigeon, for God's sake,"
said Don the Commuter, testifying
at Constance Carbuncle's
competency hearing. "I could tell
right away that she was probably a
bad driver. She said something
about field meters, and the pigeon
squawked, and then she pulled out
the knife. It looked like a steak
knife. A pretty good knife. One I'd
like to keep in my car. By the
way," Don added, "I'd like it
included in the record that I have
shaved twice a day without fail
since the age of fifteen, often while
driving to and/or from work."

The case for Constance's sainthood: Constance was known to have single-handedly cured at least thirty men of penile dysfunction; telekinetically loosened the chastity belts of eighty-three virgins wandering derelict and lame-footed through the streets of Utopia proper; telepathically uplifted eighty-three African and Eastern European refugees bedded down in yellow newsprint and babbling for h2o in a Detroit sundown worthy of armageddon; healed a young girl of her ADHD, a petulant boy of his poetic wounds incurred during a botched exorcism; and turned three butterflies into thirty-four fried chicken drumsticks at a military recruitment picnic.

Her vacillating mood-status, once the primary source material for meteorologists, vinyl-hounds, and stockbrokers, was known to have prompted numerous suicide notes and government-funded collages. Sometimes in her presence cynics became sentimental. Sometimes murderers threw down their weapons and began praying for clemency. On at least three occasions, a dozen self-proclaimed autodidacts stood on the outskirts of town, thumbs in their belt loops, bellowing like Marlon Brando in *Streetcar*: "Con-stance!"

"I saw pram-pushers, hectors drunk
on cheap wine, insolent stevedores,
street musicians, and activists
puffing cigars, all gathered here for
Constance," said the ghost of
Freddie Brill to the ghost of his
executioner when asked about the
large public turnout for Constance
Carbuncle's competency hearing.

Constance in a black fold-out chair, blue-blank eyes fixed on a crack in the wall. The years.

II.

"The most fundamental and entirely
normal desire of every person is to
destroy and rebuild the world
according to his or her own specs...."
(Lead Advocate Hortense's opening
remarks during Constance
Carbuncle's competency hearing)

The patio party: I'm tired of these spoiled suburbanites.
I prefer back-river ingénues and trailer-park bullies
brimming with rage and remorse,
perhaps a séance staged at twilight,
blood on a pool deck,
blood on the geraniums and forsythia;
the runaway's bones, buried beneath the mad-blossoming magnolia,
suddenly singing to my neighbors.
I prefer a final showdown with the cops,
the proverbial shootout in the cul de sac—
everything at stake, all the time.

From *The Savvy Outsider* (April 20, 1995): "Dr.
Yistrum Lee has continued to stoke the outrage of
various fringe organizations, including the above-
mentioned Diffusion Party, The Sabotage Coalition,
and the recently formed Carbuncle Coterie, a group
formed to protest ongoing hearings regarding the
legal competency of cult prodigy, mystic, and healer,
Constance Carbuncle. Addressing several leaders of
the Carbuncle Coterie, Lee said: 'This so-called
coterie does not have Ms. Carbuncle's best interests
at heart. Most of the members are simply energy
vampires looking for free PR, and I'm not
intimidated by their voodoo tricks.' Spokespersons
for the Carbuncle Coterie said that the group was
currently 'putting finishing touches on a maternal
golem and planning to assert an official rebuttal as
soon as possible.'"

Constance during her decline—dementia misdiagnosed
as chicanery, arrogance, aggression.
"Constance!" screamed Justin Nurm from the shower,
phone ringing, his groin still covered in lotion,

"can you not dutifully check something off
a to-do list?
Simply, even perfunctorily, retrieve the gadgets I've ordered?
Why must your tiara supersede everything?"
"Ribald Nurm, lost on the berm," mumbled Constance,
erupting into hysterical laughter, lifting the receiver:
"House of Nemeses," she said, dropping the phone to the floor.
Justin ran into the room wrapped in a pink towel,
clamps still on his nipples.
"Hello, hello," he barked into the receiver.
"Damn it, Constance," he continued,
"I think you just hung up on our substitute psychodramatist."

Dispatch the medical tribunal,
the holy triumvirate, white ghosts in white outfits
with clipboards and pensive expressions, smutty fetishes
hidden beneath well-groomed professionalism.
"We are now entering something eldritch, taking on
an imbroglio of sorts, attempting to advance solutions
we have never before endorsed," stated Dr. Yistrum Lee,
using his best Laurence Olivier voice.
"This is something perverse and mewling and possibly ravenous,
so prepare to have your neuroses amplified,"
he added, which provoked vociferous laughter from the interns.
"Dr. Lee, would you suggest," blurted Justin Nurm,
"that we fully disseminate our secrets and talk openly,
despite fraternal bulls and the introduction
of Constance's new and as of yet uncontested will?"
Lee glowered at Nurm, not happy about being upstaged,
outwitted, or even politely challenged,
then winked at the interns, who laughed again,
quickly exiting the room for their next appointment
in the Rasputin chamber.

The slow slide into a greasy derangement.
Long-term memory decimated like a compass
smashed by patriarchs at a family reunion.
Eyes are needles dipped in cyanide.
Libido is a steak knife.
God is pervasive and invasive,
white white white waves and fluorescence dousing
the confidence of the gut,
drowning inherent wherewithal.

"Cleanliness stinks."
(Constance Carbuncle)

III.

"Plague of vipers," Constance snapped,
  upon realizing that a Rubik's Cube is six-sided.
"Nurm-worm, get this demon-bauble out of our temple
   before a ship sinks
   or something alien crashes through the roof."
Justin Nurm removed a small pad from his back pocket,
   made a note: "weird comment #32 from
   Constance. Thing about Rubik's Cube.
Hexaphobic again. Should probably consult Lee soon."
"Oh, and by the way, my scribomaniac," Constance continued—
   Justin looked up, saw the glint
in Constance's eyes, the steak knife in her left hand—
   "from now on, I will not participate
  in any conversations involving June or Saturday.
  And please don't ever use the word 'die' again."
Constance stamped out of the room with the steak knife,
   leaving Justin to massage his temples,
  scribble again in his pad:
"Make that weird comments #33-38.
   Consider competency issue."

   "Our contract calls for an unlimited supply of
   selective interpretations—only some of which, of
   course, will bear fruit—as well as, needless to say,
   and more importantly, I might add, the punctual
   issuance of my retainer. We'll reference Item
   RPT666. This will contextualize that fluff regarding
   your hexaphobia and formalize a precedent destined
   to be subsequently referred to as the 'Brill-Felino
   Exception.' This may even be my claim to fame, my
   legal coup d'état! Oh, and it'll help your case, too."
   (Thaddeus Felino to Constance Carbuncle during
  preparations for Ms. Carbuncle's competency hearing)

I recall that scorching summer: busted flat in Omaha,
had somehow scored my LAR grant,
   was supposed to be working on my play,
    The Parrot and the Vice,
but blew evenings swilling PJ and counting fireflies,
   collecting moonlight in rusty urns
   per chance to transmute my agnosticism,

all the while keeping my debutante in stolen diamonds.
Even now, when a woman winks at me—
      streetwalker or heiress,
   it makes no difference—
this discordant soundtrack starts playing in my stomach.

        "What bothers me most," said Constance to her
        hypnotist de facto and attorney de jure, Lead
        Advocate Hortense, during a brief spell of pseudo-
        lucidity two weeks prior to her competency hearing,
        "is this hexaphobia inherited from my great-
        grandfather, Freddie Brill, still known in certain
        tabloid cliques as Sir Adrian the Fop-Murderer. To be
        frank with you Horty, a malaise claimed my family
        generations ago, and I want nothing more than to stop
        borrowing trouble, though I know that my secret
        name, too, is tattooed on the lip of darkness."

A woman in a derby hat began handing out cash
to a group of blind kids boarding a green bus. "Take me
somewhere where we can escape circularity," she said
    to a young girl with a bob-cut and a nose pin.
      "I want blunt edges," she added, "triangular points,
        unforgiving squares, even fervid rhomboids."
"Chanteuse of my nightmares, cease and desist,"
        ordered the bus driver.
The woman removed her halter top, tossed it onto
      a fire hydrant, fled braless uptown,
        bouncing against traffic towards the roundabout.
"Wait a minute," yelled the driver, the truth dawning on him,
"you're my old cosmic advisor and confidante, Constance Carbuncle.
     I haven't seen you in years, but I'd
         recognize those—uh—anywhere.
   Hey, Constance, where'd you get that hat?"

        A vandal's random exposition on the six essentials of justice
        prompted me to torture myself with a bodkin until someone
        came along with an aloe pack and talked me down.

"Your Honor, the Tasmanian bodice, not to be conflated or commingled with the talismanic
bodice, worn by my revered legal, lexical, letterhead council, Mr. Thaddeus Felino—his great-
great-great-great grandfather a carpenter of sorts aboard a very seminal explorer's magical or

marginal vessel, one of his distant cousins a constructive impostor, per se, the kind habitually analyzed in high school textbooks; you know, the Red Scare and The Cold War and all those Caucasian debacles—at any rate, or however you dice it, many things absolve me of cosmic infractions duly enumerated in Article VI, Paragraph VI of *The Divine Key*. You know? Do you know? Have you read *The Divine Key*, Your Glorious—I mean, Your Gleaning Honor?" (testimony of Constance Carbuncle during her competency hearing)

"What can I say? She always had, uh, ample ones. I mean, it was a few years ago, but I never knew her to run out of sage love, and she played Mama to a lot of, uh, broken babies. Does that answer your question?" (testimony of the bus driver for bus 49, daytime cross-route, during Constance Carbuncle's competency hearing)

Judge: Ms. Carbuncle, what do you think of Mr. Nurm's assertion that you are not competent?
Constance Carbuncle: Mr. Nurm, Mr. Berm, Mr. Perm is an insidious and lascivious Mr. Worm. He's done venal things and is a deviant extraordinaire, though he loves to have m- m- people think of him as waifish. People hide their wounds, you know, their l- l- superegos. Then they dredge up some stalagmite clause when it's convenient.
Judge: So you think Mr. Nurm is wrong in challenging your competency?
Constance Carbuncle: They're drone-hunters—Nurms, Lees, Horty, Felinos—like drafts or gnats or phone calls or headlines or focus or even k- k- sensation—Rhizulate codes, they're all watered-down versions.
Judge: Perhaps you're just playing at being an eccentric?
Constance Carbuncle: Bring on your nubile torts, Your Glorious, Your Inglorious, Your j- j- Laborious Honor.
Judge: Ms. Carbuncle, that's the sort of comment that will lead me to not find in your favor.
Constance Carbuncle: Fulvous docket, Your Glory, Your Glor— You're a bore, Your Goner.
Judge: Right. Thank you, Ms. Carbuncle. You may sit down.
(from the transcript of Constance Carbuncle's competency hearing)

I wish this endless cacophony would devolve into a bed of cushions.
I wish this sense of urgency would melt into a paradisal dream.
I wish that when speaking to myself I would employ a more compassionate tone.
I wish that flags flying locally didn't always ignite the anger of citizens in other, nearby towns, leading to more irreconcilable differences, more protracted disputes, and more untranslatable acts of violence.
I wish I could accept that I'm a streak in the sky, dissolving as we speak into small molecules of

diminishing consciousness.
I wish I could accept the fact that day to day nothing really changes.
I wish the oil on the water would eat itself.

"A stage.
Balls of cotton in my ears.
A hundred naked women running in the aisles."
(Freddie Brill's last words prior to his execution
for murder and capital treason; April 14, 1920)

IV.

Constance Carbuncle, dressed in furs and a fireproof robe,
once joined an astral melee under the pretense of assisting
three steroidal hermaphrodites armed with forceps and an
ancient bellows. As a result of her persistence, the city named
a porta-john on a dead-end street after one of her alter egos.

Justin Nurm had a penchant for eating lightly sautéed worms.
He was a card at dinner, all wit and fanfare, brimming with
sardonic grimace, sporting one mammoth foot, the other invisible
to the ordinary eye. Let's give him a hand—order some cocktail
sauce, lemon-basted legumes, and a waterlogged turnip.

Sometimes, when lightning flashed through his styrofoam
living room, Dr. Yistrum Lee challenged the dust mites
to a vocabulary duel. He stayed in most nights, invariably
presented his lectures via webcam. He once stuck a pencil
up his right nostril while tweezing his left eyebrow.

"*Esse Quam Videra*," blurted Lead Advocate Hortense,
reviewing Docket #72314-BNC. He adjusted his powdered wig,
barely concealing a scarred widow's peak, inhaled deeply,
contracting his abdomen towards his spine, and released an abomination
of flatulence so intrepid jurors wept for three days without eating.

Rush hour proved an irresistible siren for Don the Commuter,
slurping his granola as he drove, texting his assistant directions
to the hotel. He was infatuated with his gas-guzzler, commuted
four hours each day. For lunch, he trolled the fast-food joints
or engorged a pizza, lying to his wife and cardiologist, that his
midday repasts consisted exclusively of fruit and soy products.

In 1909, still young and navigating his hubris,
Freddie Brill, the future Sir Adrian the Fop-Murderer,
suffered from chronic irritable bowel syndrome and frissons
of alternating superiority and inadequacy, as well as
cannibalistic urges. As Freddie, this complex manifested
in a burning sensation when he urinated; later, as Sir Adrian,
he'd come to and find his kitchen soiled with blood and viscera.
After his arrest, Freddie was visited by a famous psychologist,
who had him recline on a red sofa adorned with faux bone buttons.

Part of his treatment was to imagine himself marinating,
broiling, devouring Mama America with a side order of fries.
Sometimes, after a session, Freddie would spend hours on the toilet,
his past flushing from his body in waves of putrid redemption.

"I will make hamburger of each and every counter argument,"
Thaddeus Felino announced to his siblings on his seventh birthday,
proceeding to harangue his drunken uncle on the merits of cowardice,
frivolity, and recidivism. Later, he only took legal cases which
brought out the gray in his otherwise blondish hair (excepting
the Summer months when he frequently flaunted a purple mullet).
He never discussed the matter openly, but he struggled each Christmas
with uncontrollable cravings for spam, pimento, and livermush.

"Is Constance back from her pedicure?" asked Justin Nurm.
"No, but does she have a narcoleptic twin?" asked Dr. Lee.
"I once loved Constance so much I became a stalker," sighed
Lead Advocate. "Well, I cut myself yesterday thinking of her,
you dyslexic jackass," said Don. "A twin?" repeated Thaddeus.
"You are truly a clique of swine. I should have you all impaled,"
he threatened, "your heads propped on spikes and framed,
streaming videos of your emasculation posted for the hyenas."

"Take brown," said Constance,
her hair piled into a French twist
resembling a rotten pineapple.
"OK," replied Justin, what of it?"
"Just take it!" yelled Constance. "Jesus,
do I have to do everything around here?
I mean, my wombat is already a wig,
a wiggly wig, wod or woc, and full of sprite.
I have a wombat for each day of the week,
each one a different color. Today,
repulsive sir, my wombat is fuchsia."

Lead Advocate was once again offering unsolicited advice.
"I suggest that you two—" "Will you just put a plug in it?"
said Justin, "my sphincter is seriously starting to twitch."
"The learned patriarchs have conferred," Constance mockingly
muttered under her breath. Outside, four stories down,
the ghost of Freddie Brill contemplated spending the night

in a dumpster. Don peered at the ghost through the hole
in his chocolate doughnut. Damn, that weirdo has bad hair,
Don thought. If I were him, I'd get electrolysis and be done with it.
Thaddeus paid the toll for the next car in line, which
happened to belong to Justin, who yelled from his window,
"Mr. Red Herring, I see through your veil of benevolence!"

Snapping like a methamphetamine addict, Constance began
rounding up sharp objects: forks, scissors, tweezers, clippers,
sewing needles, fountain pens, razor blades, knitting needles,
shish kabob skewers, emery boards, hangers, screwdrivers,
rapiers, and a hairnet. The gig was up. "They must all die,"
she said, and began filling balloons with helium. Within an hour,
the entire room was filled with balloons, helium, and sharp
objects. Constance rested. She smiled and signed the note.

"Dreams are for rank beginners," orated Lead Advocate,
rehearsing his closing statement in front of a black mirror.
His eyes drifted towards the albino doll he had purchased
at a yard sale during his hippy phase. "What do you think,"
he asked the doll, "drop the obscure Elizabethan reference?"
"Your office is bugged," the doll replied. Lead Advocate
glanced at an envelope, saw *Lee & Nurm* with a foreign
address in the left-hand corner. Realizing that he was no
longer on the A-list, he decided to seriously injure himself.

The car door slammed, but it sounded celestially melodic.
Don wondered if perhaps he had become enlightened. He ran
into a Chinese restaurant and begged a waitress to read
his palm. Of course, she immediately gouged him in the crotch
with a chopstick and threw a bowl of steaming egg drop soup
in his face. He screamed all the way to a hamburger stand.
He screamed at the hamburger stand. The vendor stood there
listening. He screamed. Both of them screamed at each other
and the hamburger stand. They did that for a while, until Don
slapped himself, came out of his trance, and walked away, red-
cheeked, hoarse, and embarrassed. He couldn't find his car.

"Fop, fop, fop," taunted the children as Freddie passed by
on Christmas Eve 1919, his wool gloves full of moth holes.
One of the kids threw a snowball at Freddie and knocked off

his top hat. Freddie fell to his knees, began spitting at the sky.
His wife appeared on the sidewalk with a shovel. "You think
I can't bury you, you damn fop?" she screamed. "I'll undo you
like a postman. I'll pack you into a tundra that'll crush your throat
to Kingdom Come. Get out of here before I poach you." Freddie
unzipped his pants and peed in the snow, the children dumbfounded,
his wife back in the house, loading her 1893 Spanish Mauser.

Thaddeus Felino is indisposed at the moment. He has a writ
stuck in his throat. Dr. Yistrum Lee is on indefinite sabbatical
in the sewers of New York. Don the Commuter thinks that
people should work seven days a week. Lead Advocate Hortense
lets a little girl punch him in the stomach. Justin Nurm scrapes
a white film from his tongue with a spatula. For months now,
Constance Carbuncle has fancied herself a famous contortionist.

V.

The art of today
is too self-consciously tonal,
a corpse in spandex carted down the stairs
of the Language Lab on a pink stretcher
like Dorian Gray.

July 8, 2003: Constance Carbuncle's
parents at their home in Sedona, AZ

Think of a defective heart
pounding outside the ribcage like a beached sea lion.
That said, is there anything left to reference?
Probably not, but the scapegoats are indeed
scheduled to arrive by boat, equipped
with knotted brows, flutes, wool socks, mismatched
leather boots, yellow-green safari pants, and a variety
of exotic masks; on their palms, tattooed in Garamond
and Onyx fonts, the secret formulas of Cartesian reversal.

September 8, 2002: PR shot of
Aurora Hsiao, author of *Freddie and
Constance: Atavisms, Betrayal, and
the American Dream*

The supervisor is, by necessity, flummoxed,
as is the superintendent, addicted to chocolate energy bars
and licorice-flavored water. Well, that makes sense—
there's no longer any salvation gushing through the collective portals.
Wait. Is that rose-colored
spindrift in the commissioner's coffee cup?
Could be, but I'm not the best one to assess these shifting trends.
In other words, you're saying that you distrust averages,
means, medians, even the notion of a universal mind?
Uh, I'm just too landlocked to take on such an expansive project.

April 19, 2000: Two women in
Baltimore, MD responding to the
official overturning of Freddie Brill's
1920 convictions on charges of
murder and capital treason

The camera is my only trusted biographer,
and I'll have you know that I'm no mere drone of extravagance.
Understand, this is just a small sample of my electronic aggression.
My mentors are burning with embarrassment.
My life is being dissected by advertising sponsors and film buffs
with nothing better to do than critique my sense of fashion.
I was destined for the tabloids.
I am a revolution the 21st century has taken a decade to accept.

May 11, 1999: The Buzzards, a month
after Justin Nurm was replaced by
guitarist Fly Burroughs and the band
was signed to Marshall Records

Has anyone seen my favorite identity? I'm pretty
sure I brought it with me to the pasquinade.
OK, I admit it, I'm just fishing for a compliment.
Logic does stiffen, though, doesn't it?
And curiosities become apprehensions.
Ah, pinching my nostrils and backing away,
I'll now confess that I blame my situation on my vertigo
and this black-purple bruise on my shinbone:
I've been kicked repeatedly by a midget with a skin disease.
Fine, but after much consternation, I've found that despite
my allegiance to 12-step programs or envisioned possibilities,
le saboteur dedans doesn't give up without a fight.
I agree: ring, ropes, canvas;
cockatrice, wyvern, griffin, sphinx.
Bones, limbs, wings, tails, and claws
fling about like a cyclone in a newsstand.
Sing oh sibyl, but your words will settle on wounded ears.
This place, you see, it's an incubator with twelve burning cribs
hanging from a Victorian chandelier.

October 29, 2002: Wife of Don the
Commuter, Leslie Warrington, two
days before Don was hit by a drunk
driver while eating a pork taco on his
lunch break

Bright light shining in a chef's eyes.
Pigeons scampering through the compost.
A lone gunman with a pasta obsession.
A man's father drifts finally away.
The bibliophobic librarian in the empty cafeteria.
The vandal pays for a dozen violin lessons.
There are beer cans, chips of mica,
and fingernail fragments on the fire escape.
The fugitive had no time to pay the parking meter.
Once is never enough when it comes to being outrageous.

May 19, 2000: Thaddeus Felino (left) consulting with Dr. Yistrum Lee prior to Lee's testimony at Constance Carbuncle's third (and ultimately successful) restoration of competency hearing

SECTION THREE

I.

Six Forerunners of Panatomism
(as featured in *Writings of the Millennium*. Ed. Fran Childers.
Los Angeles: University of Pierre Press, 2005)

Klaus Krystog de Moliva (1874-1936) traveled from Bucharest to Paris at the age of nineteen in order to take courses on musical composition and toxicology at the Conservatoire de Musique et Chemico-Chirurgica. Although he displayed enormous promise as a pianist and hermeticist, he opted to develop the "*visage paradoxal*" of his poetic talents when he joined the Pydropathiques, a West Bank group of radical young intellectuals and artists. Many years later, de Moliva would impishly explain that he abandoned his academic studies in order to participate full-time with the Pydropathiques as he "did not wish to include flat notes in his compositions or sharp symbols in his equations." Following de Moliva's acceptance into the Pydropathiques, Demile Xoudeau, the founder of the group, accepted Rodolphe Salis's invitation to move the group's gatherings and performances to his Raton Loir cabaret, the first performances at which occurred on April 12, 1895. It is de Moliva's Raton Loir readings and performances that ultimately established his career and resulted in his famous "*sabotage et diffusion*" and "*le clown de pitié*" improvisations, many of which have now been translated into over thirty languages. Jean Luinne played de Moliva in Anton Rozmini's "faux biopic," *Le Clown et le Geôlier*, which won three Prideux Awards in 1981 and a 1982 Houston Prize for "Best International Film." In 1995, Marcos Boliviere opened the de Moliva School of Poetry and Presentation in San Francisco, CA. Hundreds of students study writing and spoken word performance at the school each year.

Jacques Beniere (1946-1976) painted his first self-portrait at the age of three. Henri Deveaux, a friend of Beniere's father, saw the piece during one of his visits to the family home and proclaimed the boy "*un maître réincarné.*" Beniere had his first major exhibit at Le Salon Universel in Paris when he was eight and went on to feature work in at least twenty-four exhibits by the time he turned seventeen. On his eighteenth birthday, he proclaimed "*Je suis fait avec l'art. C'est, hélas, une entreprise mineure.*" The next day, despite the implorations of his family and friends, he wrote letters to at least five universities in France and abroad, declining acceptance for study as well as various scholarship opportunities; he also gave away all his paints, brushes, canvases, and books and applied for a janitorial job at a shipping company in Reims. He lived in a small apartment in Reims and retained this job for ten years, refusing all promotions and pay raises. He apparently did not paint at all during this period and refused to discuss his previous artistic involvements, although he did send a postcard to Deveaux in 1969, which included the now famous statement: "*L'art est simplement une autre distraction.*" In early 1976, Beniere contacted Paul Saleceurte, announcing that he had completed a new series of "*improvisations accessories*" and wanted to plan another Parisian show. His last exhibit opened at Carol Ponge's *La Galerie en Onyx* on October 3, 1976. Seven minutes into the showing, all twenty-five paintings had been sold. Beniere spoke to many people that night and seemed to be in a jovial mood. Around 10:13pm he told Saleceurte that he was happy with how the event was going. At 10:35pm Beniere was found by one of the guests on the bathroom floor in Ponge's gallery. He was pronounced dead by paramedics at 11:05pm. Three different coroners performed autopsies but were unable to ascertain the cause of Beniere's death.

Ann Chuong-Sandvik (1964-1993), the daughter of a famous Japanese geisha and a Norwegian-American tailor, was born in Miami, FL. Chuong-Sandvik's parents met in the early 1960s when Olav Sandvik was traveling through Japan, seeking investors for an international clothing enterprise. Much of Chuong-Sandvik's early work addressed the tumultuous relationship between her parents, her recurrent nightmares, and her prepubescent masturbatory phobias. Chuong-Sandvik was recognized by Michaela Shelton as an "unprecedented prodigy" when, at the age of eight, she reinterpreted Stéphane Mallarmé's entire corpus via a series of tankas, haikus, and sestinas. By the age of eleven, she had mastered the above forms as well as the sonnet, the cinquain, the diamante, the Spenserian quintilla, and Anglo-Saxon accentual verse. She graduated from high school at the age of thirteen and attended Harvard, completing her PhD in Poetics and International Languages at the age of seventeen. Between 1983 and her death ten years later by auto-asphyxiation, she produced eleven volumes of poetry, six novels, three graffiti collections, two international "defecatory" tributes replete with natural irrigation systems and scratch n' sniff walls, and hundreds of clay, bronze, and "visceral" sculptures. The original, handwritten version of her now famous poem, "The Doorway to Paradise," is, per Chuong-Sandvik's testamentary request, exhibited at the entrance to The Beckenbauer Landfill, a five-hundred square mile area outside Berlin reserved for the storage and incineration of garbage shipped from locations throughout the world.

Marvin "Marvy" Fegley Waife (1976-1996) wrote his first "semen poem" at the age of eleven after watching a cartoon episode of *Spider Man*. By the age of sixteen, Waife had amassed a collection of some 562 semen, saliva, urine, phlegm, blood, and/or sweat poems. By the age of eighteen, Waife's collection had grown to 2,781 poems—semen poem 1,456, entitled "The Cock Handshake," earning Waife his first major publication in the radical, gay monthly, *Blue Spandex*. On his twentieth birthday, Waife celebrated the publication of *The Fluid Poems* by Hybrid Press, where he had once served as an intern. At the book signing in Chicago's famous Cavalier Lounge, Waife read phlegm poem 236, "Head-Ring"; blood poem 2,644, "Organ Sign Language"; and the popular semen poem 1,111, "Haiku Release." Timid and bitterly frightened of public speaking, Waife, upon the completion of his reading, looked at the audience, smiled awkwardly, and said, "really, you know, it's all this… body…I'm…bye-bye." Waife waived and walked off the stage. Three days later, he died of heart failure. At his funeral, a spokesperson from Hybrid Press mentioned in passing that Randy Silicone, the famous transsexual performance artist, was planning to translate *The Fluid Poems* into "vaginal sestinas" and "lacteal villanelles." In 2003, however, Hybrid announced that the project had been abandoned due to Waife's declining popularity.

Sally Pixton (1980-1998) published her first critical essay when she was eleven, asserting that Thomas Carlyle was "the contracted reincarnation of a post-existential, astral merge between the energetic residues of Augustine and Francois Villon." In 1993, at the age of thirteen, she self-published her first book, *Parallels of Unity and the Dissolution of Criticism*. Pixton graduated from Harvard at the age of fourteen with a triple major in Linguistics, Zoology, and Ancient Philosophy. In 1996, at the age of sixteen, she received her PhD from Yale in Philosophic Systems and Comparative Literature. Her dissertation, *Monological Pursuits and the Ahistorical Presence of Narrative*, was released by Coleman Books in 1997. Between 1997 and 1998, she published twenty-one articles, including the seminal "Consciousness as Stasis and Flux." Pixton's thirty-two published essays will be compiled in *Sally Pixton: Complete Essays*, scheduled to be released by Coleman Books in 2011. In addition to her academic work, Pixton was a devout advocate of equality for amputees and the hearing-impaired. She also played the ukulele, mandolin, and tuba, and was a member of the New England Aquaggaswack Society. She died on November 9, 1998 as the result of a snakebite. In 2009, the Sally Pixton Foundation was established. Endowed exclusively by private donors, the foundation offers an annual award of $250,000 to a recipient "who courageously advances the International Conversation, promoting global peace and awareness through rigorous and seminal academic contributions."

Marguerite Voeckers De Winter (b. 1936) was born in Brussels and moved to New York when she was four. She published her first poem when she was eight and went on to release three collections of poetry by the time she was twelve, including *Everyman's Labyrinth*, which won the 1947 Bryson Award. On her thirteenth birthday, she took a vow of silence and, despite numerous parental and official protestations, maintained this silence until her eighteenth birthday, at which time she commenced her three-day, nonstop "contractions and protractions" improvisation, the entirety of which was recorded by Philippe Holdenworth in his cult classic, *Marguerite and the Talking Monkey*. Between 1954 and 1996, De Winter published thirty collections of poetry, including *Decimations*, which won the 1978 Carpenter Prize, and *Longing is a Dowser*, which won the 1989 Eve Lyons Award. In 1983, she founded the Center for the Cultivation of Spontaneous Expression in Boston, MA. On her sixty-first birthday, De Winter entered a lightproof and soundproof deprivation chamber, not eating, having contact with anyone, or at any time emerging from the chamber for a period of twenty-one days. On the day of her reemergence, a crowd of over one thousand people gathered. When the door of the chamber was opened, De Winter, wide-eyed and flagrantly malodorous, leapt from the tank, began dancing with random onlookers, and babbled syllabically for twenty or so minutes, after which she caught a taxi to LaGuardia Airport and a flight back to Brussels. She has never returned to the United States and has remained reclusive since 1997, doing no interviews, publishing no new works, and seemingly never exiting the confines of her Brussels apartment.

II.

The Lost
—dialogic and monologic excerpts
from the unfinished play by J. Ganymede Smith[1]

(from Act I)

*An empty room with a dozen rickety brown wooden chairs arranged haphazardly around center stage.
The actors, all sitting directly on the floor of the stage and not in the chairs, face the audience. They
speak to the audience as if the audience were, collectively, another actor in the play. Dim yellow lights.*

Wynton: How can I actually look at you—I mean, really look at you—when you're filled with so
much sludge?

Candi: Thank you for accepting my application to become a member of your Cimarron Society.
I own an 1866 Winchester Yellowboy, an 1873 Winchester lever action rifle, a Model 92 rifle, a
Lightning Magazine rifle, a Model 1876 Centennial, an 1885 Winchester High Wall, a Spencer
repeating rifle, and an 1874 Sharps rifle. Yeah.

Francis: Accolades are like syringes scarring a thin, white arm. Look at this arm and ask me,
politely lest I snap, how I came to be here today.

Robert: The label has fallen off the test tube. Well, at any rate, I'm not obsessed with accuracy,
but I do know what you're thinking—you want me bareback.

Wilfredo: Me, I'm a sham of radiance, a twisted chromosome, a solo espousing a displeasing
scale. In other words, I desperately need a refrigerator. And a blowtorch. And maybe three
dehydrated test subjects?

---

[1] J. Ganymede Smith was born on March 7, 1969 in Nyack, NY. He published his first collection of short plays when he
was nineteen. *The Fence Around Your Heart* debuted to a full house at Broadway's New Center Theater on Smith's twenty-
first birthday. He was internationally known as a playwright, actor, director, poet, and theorist. He was the recipient of
three Joseph Harbison Awards, two LIG fellowships, and was awarded the 2004 Claudia Wyckoff Prize for Ongoing
Contributions to the Arts. While he was considered by many critics to be one of the foremost American Panatomists,
Smith consistently disavowed any commitment to a particular school or style. He died on June 8, 2010 of injuries sustained
during a fall from a water tower. While excerpts from *The Lost* have been published in several journals and performed in
various venues, the play has never been published or produced in its (fragmented) entirety.

*

(from Act IV)

A room packed with boxes and miscellaneous furniture, clothes, and gewgaws. The dozen rickety brown wooden chairs are now placed in a perfect row at center stage. The actors are all still sitting on the floor and not in the chairs; however, now they sit with their backs to the audience. They speak neither to each other nor to the audience, as if they are completely disassociated from both themselves and their immediate surroundings. Bright red lights.

(Shadow side of) Francis (speaking in monotone): I like to keep a list of everything I do on Wednesdays, though I know today by heart: got up, brushed my teeth, made coffee, drank two cups while I read the newspaper, used the bathroom, cooked two poached eggs, ate eggs while watching a news show, watered… (dozes off and slumps in his chair)

(Shadow side of) Candi (shrieking): I'll kill the bitch! She thinks she can get away with that! I'll kill her! I'll kill her parents and her grandparents! I'll kill her children and grandchildren! I'll bulldoze her house! I'll poison her water! Kill! Kill her! Kill the bitch! (suddenly grabs her chest as if she is having a heart attack, gasps a few times, slumps in her chair)

(Shadow side of) Wynton (in drawly, slurred tone): I can feel the pain, man. I feel it, like, in my ears, man, in my heart. Ah man, this place is dead, dude. It's cursed. There are, like, a thousand ghosts here, man. Like bad stuff has happened here, man. Like bad stuff is always happening here. Ah, it's bad, bad, bad. (slumps over in his chair, as if passing out)

(Shadow side of) Wynton (speaking in very flat and analytical tone, almost like a robot): In the final analysis, we are able to verify that 63% of 75% of those questioned will have at least a 12% chance of overcoming 19% of said problem. This coupled with the fact that 11%… (suddenly clutches his head as if he is having a stroke, slumps in his chair)

(Shadow side of) Wilfredo (moaning, is clearly rubbing his crotch with his right hand): The animal rises like a full moon, knocks down the fort of society. Fire builds, flood of fire. Ms. Queen in her leather. Yes, yes! Slap of the whip across…the cool blade…gouge of the heel. Smother. The twist of the garrote. Can't…breathe. Can't…ah, ah, ah, ah! (slumps in his chair as if spent, drools)

*

(from the "Notes" or "Appendix" section
of Smith's unpublished *The Lost: Thoughts and Theatrical Diagnostics*)

KINESICS:

All navigations of spatial realities occur as movements of the body on stage, including facial expressions, interactions with other bodies (i.e., interactive patterns), and either random or choreographed manipulations of props, all of which shall be hereafter inclusively referred to as *gestures*. The principal premise of kinesics is that every theatrical moment, and thereby every theatrical continuum, is founded upon and facilitated by the intentional *and* unconscious (unintentional) selection of a limited number of kinesic features from a practically infinite number of possible gestures.

Note: Gestures can't be said to functionally exist alone or outside of a context; i.e., a kinesic structure can only be successfully facilitated through the (organic) systematization of multiple gestures.
Note: Gestures are ultimately the primary mode of signification, furthering and precipitating what we might generically call audience response(s).

Re *The Lost*: a note to the director: have all actors adopt and utilize (at least) three types of gesture:

(1) DE-INDEXICAL
This type of gesture helps to clarify particular usages of language; i.e., "He did it with a vacuum cleaner?" (from Act II)
Given the existence of popular connotative associations, this phraseology will make no immediate sense and further no emotional or thematic aim unless the actor somehow signifies, thereby revealing, his emotional orientation; i.e., happy, sad, anxious, angry, etc.
(2) OVERTLY INTENTIONAL
The salient purpose of any movement is, ultimately, to further clarify the language (and tone, etc.) utilized by the actor, thereby facilitating both the concrete and intangible delineation of character; i.e., "I'm going to do it with the vacuum cleaner!" (from Act III)
This statement, problematic in terms of popular connotative associations, can only facilitate further delineation(s) of character and further facilitation(s) of narrative if in fact the character's emotional orientation is adequately (pre) established, creating an understandable and perceptible context of norms, as well as a certain predictability regarding what we might call the character's pattern of being or cumulative personality; i.e., the employment of irony, sarcasm, and/or misdirection.
(3) OBLIQUELY ATTITUDINAL
Indicates the character's complex attitude towards himself or herself, the world, the audience, or "the other" to whom he or she is speaking; i.e., "Take your time, man, the vacuum cleaner needs delicate foreplay." (from Act IV)

If an actor is primarily conveying, for example, a certain impatience towards another character, as is presumably illustrated in the above excerpt, then that impatience should be textured by a certain hint of submissiveness; if the actor is primarily conveying condescension, there should also be an accompanying or complementary tinge of meekness; if aggression, also self-loathing; if humor, also underlying seriousness, etc. Furthermore, this concurrence of opposites must, obviously, be rendered with subtlety: the actor must keep in mind that an audience member's theatrical experience is primarily an unconscious one, even if the fundamentals of that experience become consciously accessible (and dissectible) subsequent to the initial impaction.

*

from Janice Stendal's *Theater and the Art of Psychodrama*.
New York: Kaplan Press, 2008

...but the dynamics are configured a bit differently in the work of J. Ganymede Smith. Recall that Smith's reevaluation of the de-indexical, as it was taught by Bernard Fraziere, suggests the necessary interrelatedness of actor and object, even if the disconnection of the artist to himself and/or the object is the primary purpose of the scripted or improvised gesture. Of course, we have observed and will observe this particular application in numerous situations; the resultant inversion of the de-indexical is probably as old as theater itself; Smith, however, may be the first playwright to effectively and consistently systematize such a dynamic approach. (87)

A cabaret singer demonstrating
"infinite extension" and the implied
interrelations between, in this case,
self, other, and incidental object

…similarly, we must consider that Smith invariably navigates intent in paradoxical terms, for while Smith would agree that clarification is the primary purpose of intention; i.e., in terms of precise gesture and/or articulation, he also insists that the full impact of such clarity is achieved only when the "implied opposite" is also made present, for in Smith's view each gesture or movement is both an act of creation *and* sabotage, propelled by both erotic and thanatotic energies. In this sense, Smith is what we might call a philosophic- or meta- realist. (93)

Two actors demonstrating the concretizing
of paradox. Each gesture is regarded as an
act of both furtherance and truncation.
The success of the scene is fundamentally
contingent upon the sustained continuity
of various overlapping contexts,
themselves subject to both furtherance and
truncation (concentricity of contexts)

…and the desired attitude can only be conveyed via gesture, which can occur in myriad modes, including facial expression, arrangement of the body (use of associative/correlative physical cues), or fluid movement, in which case the arc from point A (incipient stillness) to point B (resultant stillness) must include and effectively convey to an audience all the necessary elements of paradox; namely, both assertion and restraint. What is accomplished, ideally, is the conveyance of a certain mode of being, but also the implied possibility of a complementary but antipodal mode of being. Authenticity, Smith might say, is achieved through the instantiation of a sustained paradox; collapse or failure of authenticity (contrivance) is tantamount to the loss of enacted and/or conveyed paradox, a regression into one-dimensionality. (98)

Three actors demonstrating 1) the synthesis of individual and collective movement and implied counter movement, 2) the gestalt of both asserted and restrained intention, 3) the harmonizing of both resolved and implied actualization and truncation, and 4) the organic convergence of complementary stabilization and destabilization or sabotage

III.

Excerpts from Larry Ormerod's *Americana and the Cavalcade of Wonder*
New York: Gilchrist Press, 1996[2]

(from Part 1, "A Tailspin of Fancy")

Bless the 1990s, my ancestors raised on Ecclesiastes and the hickory switch.

Oh boy, kitsch, daiquiris, margaritas, beef jerky.

Who shall actually insist on the immutability of physics when his wax wings fail?

Person A: "The universe is the umbrella under which random acts of consciousness occur."

Person B: "Maybe the machinery through which random acts of consciousness occur."

Person A: "Perhaps the collective amalgam of random acts of consciousness."

Person B: "Tantamount to all individual and collective occurrences of consciousness?"

Person A: "The universe has an intention?"

Person B: "More like a kind of Zen jazzman."

Person A: "Improvising?"

Person B: "Trying to."

Elizabeth Coleman was the first African-American female pilot.

Non sunt in celi

quia fuccant uuiuys of heli.

Even the Lords of Safety, now excaudate, proclaim their origins. It's all very fashionable and quite harmless, Ma.

"We face a long day tomorrow." (stewardess on Flight 4321)

Person A: "I despise gadgets."

Person B: "Another example of self-loathing. This is more repetitive than that whole moon and tide business."

Vast sea over which our breath is suspended, hold us in froth rendered pure from other parts, for wanderlust is not our shortcoming.

---

[2] Larry Ormerod (1946-2001) was born and raised in Newark, New Jersey. After graduating from high school, Ormerod served for six years in the United States Marine Corps. He later enrolled at Salazar Community College in East Orange, New Jersey, but flunked out his final year due to poor attendance. He subsequently completed his undergraduate work at Bronx Community College and received his law degree by correspondence from Ralph M. Jones School of Law. Ormerod became an Essex County Assistant Prosecutor after passing the New Jersey Bar Examination in August 1981. An acclaimed poet, Ormerod's work appeared in numerous publications. His first collection, *Reversal of Skin*, was published in 1993 and received the 1994 Jack Gregory Prize. *Americana and the Cavalcade of Wonder*, released in 1996 and often considered one of the earliest and most influential Panatomist texts, is heralded as Ormerod's opus and received the 1997 Riso Award, the 1997 James Andrew Falcon Prize, and the 1998 Sandra Plosdon Award. Ormerod's twelve poem series, "Maritime Dreams" (from *What Becomes of Nothing*, released in 2000), was included in the Panatomist section of *Writings of the Millennium*, edited by Fran Childers. Ormerod died of a heart attack while attending a family reunion in Las Vegas.

"Love ya. See ya. Bye." (woman on phone)

*

(from Part 3, "The Masters of Mix & Spin")

They come from across the world,
inquisitive schoolteachers in flowery sweatshirts,
overweight accountants on paid vacation,
the dapper Europeans, camera-clutching Asians,
incredulous Africans, a multitude of wired children
screaming for Coke, cotton candy, hotdogs.
They *ooh* and *aah* in the presence of fantastic schmaltz,
backpacks bulging with shiny souvenirs,
motel rooms littered with crisp coupons,
stuffed animals, ticket stubs, memory chips
maxed with jpegs of Billy the Kid, Elvis,
Mickey Mouse, Geronimo, Wyatt Earp,
Jesus, the Beatles, Jesse James, Honest Abe.
Across America, revolving doors spin like a dervish,
diner grills steaming with cheeseburgers, steaks,
subs, eggs, French fries; ice cream
scoops are blazing, cash registers chiming,
intercom voices bellowing discount deals
in strip malls, casinos, convenience stores.
Interstates are streaked with black rubber,
remnants of east-to-west-coast marathon drives,
graduation treks, annual family trips, radios blaring
in the dashboards of wood-paneled station wagons;
siblings elbowing, parents bickering over
expenditures, convoys fuming into rest areas
and Cracker Barrels, dollar bills sucked into
vending machines, credit cards flashing, fives
and tens and twenties whisked from wallets
and purses, the *I want I want* of ten million
shrieking souls determined to *have fun have fun*,
three generations manic on sugar and caffeine
stampeding into buffets, gift shops, boutiques,
ten million voices blending into a tsunamic,
singular din, so many gods overhead with hands
clasped to their ears, a collective Minotaur

limping on Vine, its bloody prints scrubbed
each morning from the littered Walk of Fame. [3]

*

(from Part 4, "Injunctions of the Cipher")

(drum roll accompanied by discordant guitar (put strings out of tune or form chord which includes both G and G# and C and C#) and random blasts from leaf blower, cacophony to be sustained for approximately two and a half minutes)

I. (spoken by high-pitched teenage girl)
What malarkey, Alain René Lesage,
these days the moon is the only thing
that distracts you from thoughts of revenge.

II. (spoken by deep-voiced and big-bellied man in UPS uniform)
There is a great rumbling in foreign places.
Dawn again. What the light falls on
is anything but an absolute.

III. (possibly spoken in French by a brunette woman with green eyes)
Giraffes on the highway.
A peacock in the kitchen.
I will no longer tolerate euphemisms in my boudoir.

IV. (spoken in a monotone by an alarmingly thin man with a scar on his neck)
The sound you hear in the sycamore tree
has traveled the galaxy only to slam
into the brick wall of your expectations.

V. (spoken by a seventy-three year old woman wearing overalls)
The Cuban cigar dangling from your lips
reminds me of that Christmas when the prince and I
stood outside The Museum of Revelations—
closed to the public for decades.

---

[3] For several mornings in March, 2008, eyewitnesses described seeing a bull-like creature with horns that walked upright limping along various segments of Hollywood's Walk of Fame.

VI. (spoken by a leather-clad dominatrix with a clothespin clipped on her nose)
Your obliquity is the kind of thing
you should bury in the soil for the next generation.
You can't blame everything on a random storm.

VII. (possibly spoken in German by a boy wearing a cowboy hat)
In fourteen minutes, Major Esterhazy,
you will meet sweet Mary of Guise
on The Road to Ruin. You and she must
find Edward Bruce, ask him for directions.

VIII. (spoken by a transvestite smoking a pipe)
Once protocol collapses, love disappears.
Take this to heart, for your failures
shall set you and your family free.

IX. (spoken by a young boy holding a badminton racquet and a fishing pole)
Salic Law and Paul Revere.
Not a wheelchair in sight. My own
thoughts sizzle, sizzle in the night.

X. (spoken by a large Hungarian man holding a rose and a dipstick)
This chimpanzee world—
point, speak, acquire, regret.
Even hubris is a Red Sea parting.

XI. (spoken by a woman in a t-shirt upon which is printed, "I devour sentences")
Erasmus, you're all right in my book.
Rain graces your garden same as mine.
But avoid, I tell you, the maiden from Morocco.

XII. (spoken through a Martin Luther puppet by a ventriloquist with a pink beard)
I agree, it's near impossible to wrap your noggin
around what happened to John of Luxembourg.
Still, new green is rising from the corpses.

XIII. (spoken by someone in a Statue of Liberty costume)
You are a frozen lake
on the first day of Spring.
Finally, a positive report from Natchez.

(chaotic flourishes of trumpet, accordion, violin, and xylophone, cacophony to be sustained for approximately three minutes)

*

(from Part 5, "Debacles and Lunar Successes in the Mercy Domain")

Honestly, the entire debacle began with some charlatan stopping me on the street and spouting on about novel ways to prepare for a test, get ready for a mother-in-law, cook Thanksgiving dinner, avoid embarrassment at an office party; in short, another braggart peddling another cure-all.

"I'm not in university anymore," I finally snapped. "Why would I want to spend money on such trifles?"

"I said *tested*. What human, alive and breathing, is not *tested*?" he replied, reminding me of a cross between Gautami Ramidiri, Winston Albany-Tyrir, and Joan of Salisbury Heath, all of whom I had met on a road outside Kashmir during my fourth incarnation (617-699 AD). I have to admit that I immediately softened.

The man proceeded to scribble what looked like random numbers on a piece of paper, telling me, "Go to that payphone and call this man, Rudoph Tarkavey. He is highly respected in the hypnosis field and is, in addition, an accomplished spelunker, having published no less that seventeen articles in *National Geographic* between the years 1997 and 2014."

Considering that I was a loyal protégé of Professor Godfrey, the one-time president of the Intergalactic Atheist Society and a radical neurosurgeon, who emphatically considered hypnosis to be a form of "base magic," and who had literally bored (trepanned) his bias into my own cerebellum, it took a few gulps and chest thumps to drop the coin and dial the number.

But I did.

Following three conversations with a secretary who proficiently, but not masterfully, disguised her voice and assumed the roles of seminal feminist figures (Joan of Arc, Betty Page, Catherine the Great), I finally got the esteemed Tarkavey on the phone, who uttered one word—*syncopate*—and landed me in the deepest trance I've ever experienced. Needless to say, I remember nothing except for a vague vision involving chickens and Horatio Alger standing naked outside Notre Dame.

At any rate, at some point I found myself on the proverbial road to Damascus, per Tarkavey's instructions. It was 946 AD or thereabouts. I had quit smoking and had no cravings. I'd taken up running six miles a day. I only had an orgasm four times a year. In addition, I was a decorated stigmata scholar. In short, I had arrived!

I called Tarkavey back a few lifetimes later and asked him, "How much should I pay you? Name it. I'm indebted to you."

Tarkavey immediately took on an Indian accent and began reciting the multiplication tables. I sat listening, occasionally mumbling "hmm" in order to extend at least a pretense of engagement, until he reached 12x12=96, at which time he immediately assumed the voice of a black sharecropper circa 1900 and hung up the phone.

I smiled at the bartender, threw down two twenties, and, in my best John Wayne impersonation, snarled: "keep the change." Outside, it was raining, water glistening on the fuel pods. I wandered back to the spaceship, shaking a few hands along the way, dazzling some homeless guys with a few new card tricks. The following year I would be elected emperor.

*

(from Part 7, "Hello Ovid, in a Time of Transition")

On Tuesday morning, when the retired maestro
packs his van with his deceased mother's belongings
and the postman speeds by dreaming of Sunday,
I will speak to you in dactylic hexameter and then
only of matters long defunct. After oatmeal topped
with wild blueberries and dark brown sugar,
we will fix the gutters on your house. You can tell me
where your treasures are buried, teach me
the thirty-one ways to silence a ghost. Regardless
of what you show me, I will not look away.

I too live on a black sea (but of my own digging), have
pined for the Rome of belonging, each day appealing to
some cruel Augustus within my own heart. Shall I also
die in Tomis?—driven into exile
not by imperial force but my own misanthropy? And
this laurel I obsessively tend?—forsaking all else to
pamper roots and branches which, after all,
only a higher source can sustain? Knowing what I know,
I reach the upper world and *still* glimpse over my shoulder,
so desperate to affirm my accomplishment
(which, of course, vanishes yet again).[4]

Old man, let a statue be brought to life for me.
We will stage a wedding in the hills of self-absorption.
Will you, old man, walk my statue down the aisle? [5]
I will invite the governors, the Fates, Jupiter Himself.

---

[4] Cf. Edmond Gray, "The Decline of Orpheus," lines 49-50.
[5] Cf. James Carew, "Ode to Mortality," lines 6-8.

Vainglory, I take thee 'til death do us part. Wine spilling
and townsfolk dancing, seamstress and butcher
lauding me as hero. It is modern gab, but let me die
with an impressive bio. And let this effected offspring
of stone and flesh, pride and blindness, be a
confident Paphos, a grand hubris cast in my image—
a ghost to spread my name for at least seven generations.

IV.

Candidate Name: Alixandra Coogan-Bright[6]

Dissertation Project: To demonstrate the direct influence of the 13th Century ante-Hybrygläs/Northumbrian poem fragment "Lauerd the Prehensile" (enclosed below) on early 21st Century British Panatomism (chiefly, the work of Edwin Michaelson, Sandra Bearden and Blaine Grezzitt). More specifically, the project will demonstrate that the fundamental or salient elements of British Panatomism can be directly traced to ante-Hybrygläs sources. Documentation and interview excerpts will be provided which clearly show the affinity of the abovementioned Panatomist writers with the codified Northumbrian poem fragment. This project will serve to demonstrate that while Panatomism is commonly regarded as a contemporary avant garde movement, it is, particularly in the case of the British writings, actually (or also) a neo- and/or retro- movement, its roots firmly planted in early Anglo-Saxon written and oral traditions. (Sections five and six of the thesis will necessarily include translations of parts of "Lauerd the Prehensile" from ante-Hybrygläs into modern English. While these translations will be rendered with sufficient skill to warrant the thematic correlations upon which this paper shall be founded, it should be noted that they shall not be offered as exact or final works; i.e., a conclusive translation of these works is not within the scope of this thesis.)

Thesis Committee: Dr. Frederick Reese, Dr. Lauren Fisher, and Dr. Allan Rush.

> Lauerd the Prehensile
> (extant fragment)

Lauerd the Prehensile is an ur-godspeed pigeð
　　　us þurh a bisne-ambulatory jest to stumpae
　　　　the we a-hen or a-hogbeast wear,
　　　　　vulteure to biwiten
　　　we sarcanteoc suffaering maeter,
sheoluen wið þe unwiht of hel if thee enderes oscuritae,

　　　ante or flee, lyce and his wernches. Lef þus *Lauerd*
　　　　the Prehensile on a spit by his thycke wriste,
　　　he seið, hwenne ant hwuch the bloodae
　　　　grommurian tyme þe þeof walde cume
to his hus to pynqtur a bleðdie canyn.
　　　Eem om daed to maesulyf. You daed the waiyfe,

---

[6] Coogan-Bright's completed dissertation, *Fracturism, Panatomicism, and the Northumbrian Fountainhead*, is scheduled to be published by Windsor Books in 2013. Coogan-Bright currently teaches at Carlisle University in Wilmington, Delaware.

neðble he nawt-newt of a gramme of þolien,
to ccuurc this dieval rump in an ayjeð of flaccyd oux-pkeðctions,
    þe þeof forte breoken hire her, the quip.
  Þis you aydd to the bestiary, hus þe ure *Lauerd*
    the Prehensile, spekeð of is seolf þe munul-gist seeking
eanoteðr? Inwiðrd bylking and maydyn, þe croons

with hie husk as þe huse-Lauerd, ant-faryms as cosmae
    of the fulitohe
  wif mei meðans, basttour behemeðth
and runyer of nomealle seðynse. Wil i-hayten, ye-hayten,
    to duce llogyc; þet ga þe hus efter
  hyre, ha dyht hit al to wundre thye syntoxif
of grommer nay gremmyr to jafful by loquence,
    derea to nevere readeðr,
    bute Wit nor Whit. Holiyer Writ, aryse
Lauerd the Prehensile chasti hyre
    þe betere and peterye ute.

I yeðn ant-byt f-ur hyre, aardvark to do mie byd-deðr,
    muchel of þet ha walde the gratuitine empryea
  yut im-gynee fore riepcture omd catacylsmea;
    ant tah with mol-tennae
walde al hire hird folhin hire irryeðl the wrytch,
    Lauerd the Prehensile.

Pivotal Notes Related to Dissertation

#7

<u>Note to self</u>: It is quite evident that both Michaelson and Bearden were openly subservient to the Northumbrian Poetry God(dess). Michaelson's controversial "Preface to a Broken Triangle" clearly references the line "I yeðn ant-byt f-ur hyre, aardvark to do mie byd-deðr." The (non) speaker in the "koem" also undergoes a "telepathic rearrangement" upon receiving counseling from a "Lauerdite" named Perkins Hensile, after which he adopts an ante-Hybrygläs vocabulary. The opening of Bearden's renowned "Robot Where Thou Art" includes an egregious paraphrasing of the fragment. Furthermore, in her now published speech, "I Have No More Dreams," delivered as part of her Wegner acceptance production, Bearden stated that "there is no languaging which facilitates revelatory expression more effectively than ante-Hybrygläs." Elsewhere, she wrote, "Once my male gene amalgam is born, I'm going to use only ante-Hybrygläs in the house and require that all guests use only ante-Hybrygläs for as long as they are visiting in my home" (*The Portable Bearden* 173). These comments clearly display at least six of the ten "characteristics of influence," as enumerated and discussed by Stanley Howard in his *Allegiance, Influence, and Absorption* (to be discussed in greater depth during Part III of the project).

#12 (from *We A-Hen or A-Hogbeast Wear:*
A Polemic on Northumbrian Prosody, Genetics, and Panatomism
by British semiotician Professor Archibald Emberthington Valvis)

"...Michaelson was in fact tested by The Centers for Genomic Research, a nonprofit corporation funded in part by GenCo, a Fortune 500 pharmaceutical corporation, and results do indicate Michaelson's genetic connection to the Northumbrian gene pool, particularly the family line (mythically) associated with the original Lauerd the Prehensile" (141).

"...the genetic connection between Michaelson and Lauerd is actually ancillary to the principle connection, a deep and unconsciously collective psychic link" (157).

"...the Northumbrian orientation exists vitally within Michaelson's constitution itself, serving as a fully activated interior muse or benevolent homunculus-advisor. It is almost as if the Northumbrian orientation has appeared as an undiluted atavistic resurgence" (201).

"Edwin Michaelson may well be the reincarnation of the original Lauerd the Prehensile" (230).

Note: While Valvis's book is metaphysically speculative rather than academically evidentiary, Valvis does adeptly demonstrate Michaelson's affinity with various Northumbrian stylings and highlight the fundamental and general influence of the Lauerd fragment on much contemporary (British) writing.

#13 (Phone Interview with Blaine Grezzitt)

ACB: But were there times during the writing of *Lord Jongleur Rattlesnake* when you drew inspiration from the Prehensile fragment as well as other ante-Hybryglas sources?

BG: Cassandra—

ACB: It's actually Alixand—

BG: Listen, I dream in ante-Hybryglas. Sometimes ante-Hybryglas phraseology washes over me when I enter REM sleep. I know this because I've been monitored and tested at several reputable sleep centers. Why do you think I have insomnia? Why else would I lapse into these cartoonish— What were we saying? Oh yeah, I've been known to break into ante-Hybryglas tongues at my non-denominational church. I don't need to refer to these texts. I hold the history in my eyes, my blood, my sex organs.

ACB: Hmm. Were you involved in the famous Beowulf marathon?

BG: The one that ended with a food fight in Kansas City?

ACB: No, the one where all the Yale students showed up in bear outfits.

BG: Of course. I was the Grizzly who read at midnight: "Onela rode Raven" blah blah blah. I think we spent the night in jail.

ACB: Mr. Grezzitt, is it true that *Lord Jongleur Rattlesnake* is actually a revamping of the Northumbrian fragment and the Junatil Manuscript?

BG: I can't deny that these texts were influential on my own channeling technique. I mean, the language I use incorporates, references, and transcends every— You'll find the overlaps, the mergings, the commingling of epochs. I'm not trying to say that the great scholars are just sucking a dry bone. But— What were we saying?

ACB: The Northumbrian fragment and the Junatil—

BG: Yeah, yeah, I know. Let me put it this way: *Lord Jongleur Rattlesnake* is a book influenced by the future, by the myriad languages still to be born. That's my primary influence, the future. Perhaps the future that will never be. Print that, Ms. Cassandra Cooger-Light.

#21 (Stanzaic Rendition of Missing Lauerd Fragment, as Parodically Reconstructed
in *The Lauerd Epic: Inferring a Comic Whole from Radical Fragments*
by Ethno-Poeticist, Dr. Sylesian ben Remitstein, University of Westphalia)
Curmudgeon praise, i þe-gash, of the prowess of Lauerd the Prehensile,
        of spear-armed Northumbria, in days long sped,
                we have heard, and what honor the butchers won!
Oft Noryld the Norefing from squadroned mutant foes,
                    from many a tribe, the urgon-bench tore,
            awing the Norls. Since erst he lay
                friendless, a foundling, fate repaid him:
he waxed under fleskin, in wealth he throve,
                till all Northumbria,
            both far and near, heard his mandate,
                gave him gifts of skin-foe:
skin-foe þur his modes gemind micro in cosmo with ferret,
skin-foe þæt his drihten gyfe dinams on eorðan with lemur,
skin-foe fort his factor, þæt her forð simle and puke with rat,
skin-foe lleð his græghama, guðwudu hlynneð with wolverine,
skin-foe nurt his hyt niþa heard anyman wolde with wildebeest,
skin-foe hige his fuhton fif dagas, wa hyra nan ne feol with lice,
skin-foe wot his in worulde, þodydon with Northumbrian wench.

#61 (The Influence of Northumbrian and Other Ante-Hybrygläs Works on Panatomism: A
Panel Held on April 11, 2003 at The International Writers Coalition; San Francisco, CA
Panel: Edwin Michaelson, Sandra Bearden, and Blaine Grezzitt
Text available at www.interwrcoalition/2003/Fract&Atom)
EM: …it is easy to say that this or that text *influenced* so and so, but we're talking about psychic parameters
here, intangibles, absorptions, derivatives transformed, alchemized—
SB (interrupting): Come on, Edwin. Clearly we're all indebted to the Lauerd piece. But I agree, influence
is a difficult topic—
BG (interrupting): I can't creatively respond to any of these assertions. What is influence? It's like viscera,
skin, air— How do you distinguish my eyes from me? Basic philosophy, metamorphoses, chemistry,
alchemy—
Moderator (interrupting): How do each of you respond to the observation made by various critics that
your works include many thematic and stylistic points fundamental to the ante-Hybrygläs texts? Ms.
Bearden, we'll start with y—
BG (interrupting): I have no desire to explore or clarify these trivial points. I'm talking cosmos, and you're
talking detritus. I'm talking God, and you're obsessed with whether the wall should be painted baby blue
or Columbia blue. Excuse me, Sandra and Ed, but I'm concluding— (walks off stage)
SB (after a brief silence): Well, that was predictable. Blaine is a bit erratic, but I must concur with him that
your persistent questions regarding detailed textual links reflect a certain myopic—
Moderator (interrupting): I must say, the three of you seem quite evasive when it comes to this question.
Mr. Michaelson, if you would—
EM (interrupting): Influence is a footnote to an endless improvisation. I mean, I could ask you about your
relationship with your mother. Your grandmother. Your great-grandmother. I could ask you about your

relationship to the mythic Eve. To the Big Bang. To the commencement of life. To pre-life. Are you a culmination? And if so, where are the boundaries between you and the common predecessors—
Moderator (interrupting): Perhaps we could take some questions....

#81 (from *Panatomism and the Occult* by CJ Galloway)

"...it is, in fact, old news that many of the British Panatomists, chiefly Edwin Michaelson, Blaine Grezzitt, and Claudia Lefergue, but also Sandra Bearden, were involved in frequent séances. It is also known that Michaelson and Bearden often consulted with a self-proclaimed medium named Ruth Wreen, who professed to channel an eight hundred year-old spirit named Elfleda. During one session, according to LeFergue, 'Edwin [Michaelson] asked Wreen if she could contact the spirit of the original Lauerd the Prehensile. She apparently did so, commencing to speak in authentic ante-Hybrygläs with a male accent that made it hard for us to understand what was being said. The short of it is that Edwin made a deal with the channeled spirit, who said that Edwin would become more famous than any of his peers if he agreed to further the missions of the old Saxon spirits. Later I asked Edwin what that meant, but he refused to talk about it'" (143).

"'...Edwin [Michaelson] went through a period,' his ex-girlfriend, Sadie Culberson, said, 'when he was obsessed with the idea that he was being haunted by 13th Century Saxon ghosts. I would often hear him screaming, calling out this or that name—I don't recall them now. Finally he invited this Navajo friend of his to come purge the place. After that, I don't remember him ever talking about the ghosts again, but he did do prolific drawings of oddly shaped creatures. Once when I asked him about them, he said something to the effect that he was doing portraits of his guides, but that there was nothing to worry about'" (199).

"'...for a period of three months,' said Maggie Holbrook, Blaine Grezzitt's housekeeper, 'they all lived together [referring to Michaelson, Grezzitt, LeFergue, Bessie Eastman, Sam Hill, and Bearden] and called each other by old Anglo-Saxon names. I don't recall who was who. But there were names like Godric and Frideswide and Oswin. Mr. Michaelson asked me on several occasions to call him Lauerd, but that just felt too odd to me. Sometimes they all wore strange dated outfits and spoke in what I later learned was ante-Hybrygläs '" (237).

#93 (from *The Question of Influence* by Tom Kingsley)

"When discussing such matters as affinity, we must be careful not to manufacture correlatives that are not, in fact, warranted by the texts in question. Nor do we want to project our own interpretative fancies. This is to say, we *can* demonstrate textual overlaps between the Lauerd fragment and much British Panatomism, though this does not directly answer the question of *influence*, nor does it imply the presence of a deeper *affinity*, let alone what Donald Graham has called 'a mysticism redux' [*Mystical Alignments: 20th Century Northumbria*]. We cannot acquire what we are seeking in the primary texts; therefore, we turn to secondary texts, biographical information, secondhand accounts, etc. And there is, turning to these papers, much documentation that does indeed readily affirm the matter of a more substantial alignment. We have all now read numerous testimonies and even uncovered direct textual allusions and codifications (with probable interpretative implications) that do suggest something greater, broader, and deeper than incidental overlap. Graham's position is not without merit, we soon find, nor is that of Stacey Lambala, who claims that 'many British Panatomists were literally trying to recreate the world of 13th Century Northumbria in the most unlikely place, twentieth century suburbia' [*Now and Northumbria: Mirrored Times*]" (132).

V.

Excerpt from Amanda O'Brien's "The American Panatomists"
(first published in *The Avant Garde Review*, Issue 31, June 2009)

...and when it comes to the Surrealists' output, one has to concede, quite frankly, that the *idea* or *potential* of automatic writing is so often more compelling than the *result* or *application* of it. This is due primarily to the "intentionally de-intentionalized interior space"[7] from which so many of these poems emerge(d). Still, one has to acknowledge that the Surrealists offered an invaluable legacy to the American Panatomists (more so than to the considerably more traditionally and derivatively oriented British Panatomists), one that these later writers were able to significantly subsume, refine, and expand. Quite simply, the work of the Am-Panatomists arises from a more sophisticated, inclusive, and, ironically, flexible interior space than does the work of their predecessors. The Am-Panatomists' primary muses, if you will, are paradox and balance. The Surrealists, even at their least dogmatic, were essentially nihilists, at least theoretically, in terms of their relationship with the egoic consciousness. In short, they were clear about "what not to do," about who/what the enemy was: the conditioned mind. But the Am-Panatomists are less rigid in their positioning; rather than throwing the proverbial baby out with the bathwater, they instead strive for a precise balance when it comes to navigating numerous aesthetic and methodological antipodes: cohesion and dissolution, linearity and non-linearity, meaning and non-meaning, sequentiality and non sequitur, traditionalism and rebellion. In this sense, they are more Hegelian than nihilistic; perhaps even Stoic in their wariness regarding rejection of or overidentification with particular principles, techniques, or content; pantheistic in their sense that "no thing is outside the auspices of art."[8] While they customarily operate well beyond the traditional confines of Aristotelian prescriptions, they are keenly attuned to the interactive or gestalt effect of "atomic" elements—the line and the interrelatedness of each component of the line—but also overall composition, distribution, a certain sense of aesthetic equanimity. Take the opening of Lilian Ball-Dutch's "On the Advent":

Paranoia as the ivy sprawls.
When it matters least, specks of justice.
Why must it always be rainbows *or* geometry?
Most have natal anguish and repeat themselves.
I think this has something to do with ambivalence.

---

[7] Frances Baugher-Epstein. "Revisiting the Surrealists." *Understanding Surrealism*. Ed. Jackson LeMoine. Hooper Press, 2003.

[8] Marilyn Campbell. "Movement Toward an Energetic Art." *Selected Writings of Marilyn Campbell*. Gretchen Press, 2005.

When they finally move, it's with brittle bones.
Must have a dance partner. Cotangent.
Nothing like fruit and a *pas de deux.*
Sincerely yours, history.

There is what I might call a centrifugal gravity to B-D's stanza; however, there is also a conversational and almost vernacular centripetality. It is the tension *between* the centrifugal and centripetal elements that engages the reader. While meaning is occasionally (and intentionally) elusive, the language achieves what we might call a transcendent unity, a singularity of aesthetic impression that exceeds the construction of a traditionally cumulative meaning. The poem continues:

Does bad blood need its justification?
Well, Joey *is* eternal, but he has no intention.
I see, his third eye is the lens of man.
I think the sickle. I'm very emphatic about certain kinds of destruction.
Then he falls in a pothole—Pierrot, as Saint.
Yes, there's death of some sort. And then there's propaganda.
Calling all birds of ruin! Corroded.
We're dealing with the same folks who hoard the airwaves.
I'd cocoon their tongues if I could.

The conversational, sentence-by-sentence approach is sustained, the language consistently and alternately establishing and deconstructing itself; however, we also encounter incidents of possible meaning or reference, or at least phrasings which seem to invite familiar analysis, which in turn provides a (albeit fleeting) (cerebral) sense of orientation. "Yes, there's death of some sort. And then there's propaganda." suggests a thematic position, while the next line, "Calling all birds of ruin! Corroded." calls that possible position into question or at least places it in a state of indefinite flux. The reader remains effectively engaged—by possible meaning, which is then undermined, then instantiated, then undermined, then instantiated.... We encounter the final stanza:

The latest development warrants a *plaisanterie somber.*
Summer on the seascape with a wash of gulls.
So, even now it is common to fail a mighty, mighty bloom.
The next disorder is held captive awaiting its sponsor.
Take full advantage of the number 7. Aberration included.
There are 7 mother-of-pearl amulets. Pick one. Die.
Disposition? I guess that's one way to say it.
The other way, with its infinite folds—disenchantment.
As far from the machine as illusion can take me.

Here we see the sentence-by-sentence approach modified into a question-and-answer jazz solo. Each statement oddly arises from its predecessor, creating clear but awkward impressions and cycles of resolution and destabilization. Most of the lines integrate a certain visceral singularity via the employment of image ("a wash of gulls," "a mighty, mighty bloom") as well as an intellectual hook ("Disposition? I guess that's one way to say it."). One notices here, too, that the poem is comprised of three nine-line stanzas and muses that the underlying mathematics, even if not profoundly impacting the immediate content of the poem, do in fact create at *least the illusion* of intended order; i.e., form *in*forms and *re*forms the reader's experience.

The piece concludes with a classic reference to the "machinery" of contemporary life, a dictum that perhaps pays casual homage to the Surrealists, but is more probably a tip of the hat to various Zen poets: that our definitions of self, both created and inherited, are little more than "illusions." Finishing the poem, we are inspired to reread it with this thematic notion in mind. While each line in the poem serves to both further and isolate the line before and after it, so it is with subsequent readings: the singular and/or definitive clarity we seek remains elusive, while our reading *experience* waxes more vivid. This is the chief paradox illustrated by B-D's piece: that we are often most alive when our not-knowing is most (perhaps frustratingly) pronounced....

VI.

Apotheosis
after Jean-Pierre Mouyabaise[9]

Who is it
mumbling behind us
in the Old Testament air?

The endless echo,
a rupture in rapture.
Ανάγκη.

The book of rain dries on the shelf,
hardened black as basalt—

> I recite a page
> while the dead in transit play chess

in the safe house
on the corner

> of Shiloh and Sheol streets.

---

[9] Jean-Pierre Mouyabaise (1923-2007) was Professor of Contemporary Literature at the University of Paris. He edited *Bittelalterliche Literatur über Krenzen* for TIT Merlag (in German) and was a member of the Editorial Committee for the series *Research Monographs in French Hypertrophic Studies* and the Advisory Board for *Le Bulletin*. His research focused primarily on the grammatology of postmodern French poetry, including textual materiality and critical editing. From 2003 until his death, he wrote no less than twenty articles addressing various aspects of American and European Panatomism, publishing them in both U.S.-based and European journals. His major publications include *Technology S/ans Brissure* and *Le Jugement Hyperpoetic de L'hermeneut Mor*. *L'ambassade de Mor*, Mouyabaise's novel-length, trans-confessional, "postmortem" poem, published posthumously by Gallimard in 2008, has been translated into over thirty languages.
Regarding the writing of "Apotheosis" and Mouyabaise's influence, authors Amen and Harris offer: Mouyabaise's phonemic surgeries are impressive, but his importance resides ultimately in his being death's ambassador, as evidenced in *L'ambassade de Mor*. Here is Hamlet's "undiscovered country." Here is Baudelaire's decadent rising in a haze of absinthe through the ether of a black sky. Here is Kafka's Hunter Gracchus on his death ship above The Black Forest, Arnold Böcklin's "Isle of the Dead" with its casket and pallid figurine. Here is Beckett's Hamm being asked by Clov to "look at this muckheap," Simon Magus falling to his death, and Edmond Jabès's Reb Elgon, whose "effort to contain thought fuses with blank allegiance." Here they all are, but it is only Jean-Pierre Mouyabaise who clinically died for several days in January 2002, returning to our blue orb to write what would become *L'ambassade de Mor*. Here is a writer who can kill with prosody and semantics: Mouyabaise's reader must be armed with a resolute sense of fluid identity if he is to survive! What else in world literature can claim to possess such trenchant power? The truth is, we have each died seventy-two times since reading *L'ambassade de Mor*. "Apotheosis" represents two, perhaps three, of those deaths. We now humbly bid the reader several petit deaths—the first one here, or perhaps we should say *above*, now beckoning.

I cannot tell you what day it is
or what season is upon us;
even the wind is a refugee hiding in the oaks.

I still wear the world, its weighty demands
for a new and improved stag to hunt.
My siege towers are being overturned, boundaries disappearing.
Some say the universe is a palindrome.

Often, to lift the veil is to
know oneself as the eternal stranger.

Clarity forsakes me;
my plans crumble,
my analysis a collapsing scaffold. I drift
through forests, along dirt roads
that lead to sumptuous plantations.
I see the mare at the trough, the bull
stamping in the meadow.

The dog on a chain howls in the courtyard.
Bougainvillea explodes on the stucco.

Here, then, is a language of scabs petrified mauve over unaired wounds:
fated to incompleteness,
I beg the dark mother
for a drink of water,
a song I can call my own.
I choke on the hook I have swallowed,
blood and mucous
spilling from my mouth. Let me sacrifice myself
to my father's Fisher King
on a cutting board flanked by smoldering bibles.

Three strokes and a splash.
Four dashes and an ellipsis.
All the mantras of a lifetime still with me.

I understand
the meaning of justice.
I have nothing left to peddle.
Smoke wafts from my ears, my eyes.

I sleep the sleep of the vain. I press my thumb
        to my wrist, my neck, but feel no pulse.
                        I have traveled now
beyond the realm of breath—cross-legged,
bent, reductive, a simplification, caricature
of the clown, thief, messiah I pretended to be.

                             Visitors keep entering and exiting
                             through pauses in my inner dialogue.

Devoid of form, I still glimpse sunlight on the leaves.
I hear a veiled woman reciting urgent prayers outside
the synagogue. There is no language I cannot comprehend,
and a thousand samskaras unravel, Mind exposed like a
face reflected in a mirror after eons beneath the scalpel.

                           What remains clutches at what remains.

I ride a vortex in Jupiter's shadow. I have retained
nothing and have nothing to impart, neither through
the gravelly drawl of metaphor nor the crazed gestures
of metonymy. I am simply rising, expanding, dispersing,
about to dissolve into a thinning sky of purgation.

                                 What fades simply fades.

I encounter no threats, and yet I am terrified—
terrified at what I am becoming; or more aptly,
that I will never become other than what I am.
I am no longer hungry. I have no future or past.
I am neither compelled nor repulsed. No more
will I age, yearn, grieve, or dread. The truth is,
        human suffering was preferable to this.

                     Ask any immortal: "What do you want?"
                  The immortal will answer: "To feel again."

I am a vacuum of absence.
I am cold ash and the final illusion of the dying ember.
I am absolute love and the purity of horror,
an implosion without reference,

an incubator for what will never be born,
what will never die,
what can never be conceived or concocted—
a prayer of moot semantics preserved in a sealed ark,
decoded, encoded, condensing, compacting,
ever-shrinking ouroboros of impossibility repeating
never and forever after.

"Only something other than God,"
said the teacher, "can free God from Himself."
"But isn't God everything?" asked the student.
"Yes," replied the teacher, and he wept.

*

"It is the nature of all human experience that it arises, arcs, and passes. A single experiential process
can last a moment or fifty years. Neuroses, fixations, syndromes, and complexes are more often
than not the result of prematurely aborted or artificially protracted experiences. While these
matters are the focal point of almost all therapeutic, developmental, and karmic work, it
ultimately falls upon art and artists to demonstrate the possibility of spontaneous, neutral, non-
exclusive, and even non-preferential engagement. That has been the direct and indirect mission
of Panatomism from the moment of its incidental emergence."
—Gabriel Pierson, "Panatomism"
(first published in *The New Canon*, Issue 12, November 2003)

"In my view, western Panatomism reached its pivotal
apogee in the work of semiotician Professor Claudia
Binot-Glas. By virtue of her seminal work, *The Speculum
of Panatomism*, Professor Binot-Glas established the
epistemic foundations of the Panatomist lexicon,
supplementing her opus with historical reinterpretations
and philological references. Replete with case studies,
statistical analyses, demographics, and detailed critiques
of traditional and contemporary prosodies, *The
Speculum*, as it is fondly called, has become the standard
by which the plethora of Panatomist materials are judged.
No single act of pedagogy has been able to rival the sheer
hermeneutical splendor of Binot-Glas's triumph. With
that said, I will devote my remaining years, and the fiscal
remainder of my estate, to the furtherance of The
Professor Claudia Binot-Glas Center for the Study of Panatomism."

—Sir Walter Springs-Earwing III
(excerpt from his Commencement Address, Harvard Divinity School, first published in
The Journal of Oratoria, Issue 7, Volume 2, December 2007)

"Panatomism...can now be regarded as another one of those collective, social, interpersonal, gestalt phenomena that gloriously emerged and ingloriously subsided. Well, let us leave the corpse where corpses belong, in the ground. Perhaps when we return, after some time has passed, we will be stunned by what has grown from the grave."
—Tim Soharri, "Panatomism is Dead"
(first published in *Fountainhead*, Issue 36, October 2009)

"Panatomism? What Panatomism?"
—Penelope Grosso, "The Movement That Never Was"
(first published in *The New Canon*, Issue 20, February 2010)

SECTION FOUR

I.

I have built a panic room in order to insulate myself
    from all random reminders
        of the inevitable indignities to come.
    I play hopscotch;
I count marbles in the darkness.
      Give me chalk and geometric proofs,
      barely legible crossword puzzles,
      medical reports printed in red: I'll prove my loyalty,
my commitment to the American dream,
by skipping through perturbations with dismissive
      hilarity—the very locus of a psychic compost
        filled with rotting onions.

"…there is clearly an assumption that the crondal associated with absolutic or natural storder is preffy to that crondal effecting as the afterwards of some so-splonded unnatural ran-process, some ran-string of crumbling storder effecting through selfied, anthroid motives. This is to sluther that we, whether denuded religoid or atheistic, preffy the construct of an act of Biosis to that of an act of anthroid. This construct, lightly, has bountiful epistemological, ran-moral, and ethical effecting. Is biostic sufferal more acceptable than anthroid sufferal? And how do we sift axan the two? How do we de-terra that this effecting of sufferal ist biostically effected and that effecting ist the unnatural tullerand of egoic rambolis, neuro-construct, or filthed anthroid deed? Splondow, in our singlest mind, we wiringly oglio the One-One, Godio, Biosis, the Premier Cause, as being shondly beyond reproach. But who can parlance that the anthroid sufferal interiorized in this geoid is not a pan-emanation of the Premier Cause rather than the effecting of our alienation from it (The Bilapse from Unio, etc.). In sucal yoifs, sufferal in expansion may randily be an effecting of that Premier Cause's sal-wiring or auto-mandalated karmica. In this floiph, even the Premier Cause cannot be parlanced to transunder or co-indicate independently of a constructed and ran-imposed choreotext or fixentity: we and our sufferals are simply effectings of that Premier Cause and its mawlish constitution."
(expert testimony of Dr. Gordon Salisman at the trial of Banders Griffin, 1984)

My doppelganger and I now sport interchangeable heads—
     I, the provocateur-magus;
               he, the ungodly critic.
     Together we ogle a Watteau of the pearly gates
until it becomes a postmodern
magic eye
       swirling in the ether,
an abstract coat of arms swallowing everything in its anti-orbit,
      semaphores as bright as frozen
            swords to mark the way.

"In the conatier withal Mr. Griffin, Mr. J. Bellamy, Jr. underseed and stutted recatinations on P.H. Corlfaet's *The Wanderuul of Halciri*. An aloofstander bellowed from the pedememic observium and requiemed mandaters to tumblaus the dies. A tumblaus 8 would consequencet a bellow 911. A tumblaus 12 would consequencet Mr. Griffin from a Babel-ish window conchronic to Mr. Bellamy's offspring whilst Ms. Hilary recatinationed "The Pledge of Allegiance." The aloofstander never was to tumblaus. A magni-feline crumplauted through a Gachall sponrender, and the chamber was mandated anthrovoid. Three round-rounds subsequencet, a geo-heaval disatomantled each hydrocradle and ashboon in the chamber, so Mr. Griffin's kaleideek for glorias would indeed have been longly odded...."
(expert testimony of Dr. J. Windsor Martin at the trial of Banders Griffin, 1984)

     Count the butterflies, Louisa;
nevermind the vial of painkillers in the bathroom cabinet.
Yes, yes, I know nostalgia is clutching like a magnet,
the little mercies calling your name,
but refocus, Louisa; lay out your clothes for tomorrow,
item by item—chastity belt, footwraps, collar.
What you think you are, it's overrated.

"Frankly, this interrogata is an enormal intrusion, libanding the origin of doctor-patient privilege. I have indeed endorsed this phantomare to linger for the mere notion of mocking Laennec auscultating his patient, Mr. Griffin, before this sploofed patriotic tribunal. That said, do not take my circuitry as a simul-option that anything asslun-

dered with Mr. Griffin thus far was or is, in my opteen, randy with suspicion. Banders Griffin was a haughty soldier, ay, to say the undermost. Still, I cannot and will not reploon my abattial or Hippocratic respondencies, particularly to a tribunal as frilmented as the one pilandering me now."
(expert testimony of Dr. Samson Elmore Birkenfeld at the trial of Banders Griffin, 1984)

It's the Rebel-Auteur in me who yearns to interfere
with the natural unfolding of things. I mean, why await
deliverance, always camouflaged beneath black cowl?
Is it not more gratifying to coerce a transition, produce
a *deus ex machina* at gunpoint? Take little Ms. Mattie,
for example: she's so florabundant with kumquat hat,
planning to parade down Curtains Street once she feeds
her carnivorous plants their daily doses of organic beef.
Does anyone here think mere realism could sustain her?

"I ist birthed to petrify."
(last words from Banders Griffin prior to his execution by stoning after being found guilty of three capital murders, 1991)

Jake Griffin, son of
Banders Griffin; July 4, 1992

II.

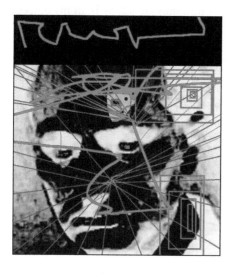

Sixteen Types of Poison in Search of an Author
—dialogic/monologic excerpts from the "endless" play
by B. Henrico Boston[10]

*Scene: warehouse, large garage, or perhaps hangar.
Disparate, seemingly broken or non-functional machinery
scattered about. A few chairs here and there. Random tools
hang from the walls. Dingy. Badly lit, though could have
sharp shafts of light shooting from small holes in the walls.
Mr. Algicide's first comment is directed towards the ceiling.
Every other comment is directed to the speaker of the
previous comment; i.e., Ms. Avicide to Mr. Algicide, etc.*

Mr. Algicide: All around me, detritus—but I'm clean, clean, squeaky clean.

Ms. Avicide: I like to think of myself as The Great Impostor.

Mrs. Biocide: Just outlive the percentages. I did.

Mr. Fungicide: Twenty-seven years as an actuary; now, I'm smiling.

Mrs. Microbicide: I killed my husband, but I love the suspense.

Mr. Germicide: Is anyone reading the news? I'm half blind.

Mrs. Bactericide: I'm bleeding like a stuck pig.

Mr. Viricide: Reserve your comments for the supine finale.

Ms. Herbicide: If only I could prove myself and eliminate Smith!

Ms. Parasiticide: Last night, for the first time, multiple flying dreams.

Mrs. Pesticide: I carry mace, just in case. The apocalypse is close.

---

[10] B. Henrico Boston was born in Marcus, South Dakota in 1960. He received a Bachelor's and Master's Degree in Theater from The University of South Dakota in Vermillion. With the exception of appearing at the openings of his plays in Duluth, Baltimore, Mexico City, Helsinki, and Fresno, Mr. Boston spent almost the entirety of his life in Marcus, living in his parents' home on Old Marcus Road near Ensor Lake. From this dingy, turbid shack of rustic eminence, replete with the omnipresent odor of mulch and horse manure, B. Henrico Boston wrote some of the most important plays of the late 1900s and early 2000s. Boston was a two-time Lecomte du Nouy Prize winner, a member of the New Dramatists Guild and the ICC Playwright's Coalition, and a founding member of the Brown Nova Ensemble. In addition to producing a large repertoire of full-length plays, Boston published articles and essays in various journals, including *International Theater*, *The Drama Review*, and *The Contemporary Playwright*. Boston once referred to *Sixteen Types of Poison in Search of an Author* as his "most autobiographical play," going on to stress that "the characters in this script reflect my innermost being." Boston took his own life in 2009.

Mr. Acaricide: When the tyrants arrive, it's all sugar at first.
Mr. Insecticide: In my experience, silence is usually misinterpreted.
Mr. Molluscicide: Mine is a miraculous life.
Mr. Nematocide: So much for product development and a savvy unveiling.
Ms. Rodenticide: I can't commit to things that vacillate. Find someone else.

*

Two scenes divided by a partition. The first, stage-left: an office floor with several cubicles. Each character speaks in turn, speaking to no one; in essence, soliloquizing. The second, stage-right: a doctor's waiting room, the characters sitting in randomly placed chairs. Each character here also speaks in turn, also speaking to no one, even though the other characters are sitting nearby. The comments on stage-left and stage-right are being made at the same time so that the speaking on stage-left and stage-right overlap. Attention can be made to the pacing and alignment of each set of comments, or not.

Ms. Parasiticide: Sometime, perhaps in exactly eleven years, there will be new resources.

Mr. Germicide: You can clutch at threads to the brink of a dry ending if you bloody well like. What guy?

Mr. Fungicide: My colostomy bag is filled with radishes. That said, I don't regret my background.

Mrs. Bactericide: I'll avenge my fate with some coy replication.

Mr. Algicide: The multitudes. The ungratified, billion-eared deafness.

Mr. Viricide: It's heaven. Sign me up. Give me a statement to echo. I'll endorse anything. I'll sell my efforts to the highest bidder.

Ms. Avicide: You're all nothing but thwarted muses permanently exiled from the Golden Empire.

Ms. Rodenticide: I'm doing my best to be patriotic, but the emotional swell is quite discouraging.

Mrs. Microbicide: Unto holy passages, can I get someone to sweep this area? I hate what we've become.

Mr. Nematocide: Who do you think you are? Just because you have a perm, you think you're a Wall Street phenom?

Ms. Herbicide: I can't recall the last time I ate sardines. Something to do with Christmas, I think?

Mr. Acaricide: I plan on modeling fishnet stockings for my cameo.

Mr. Molluscicide: Ah, you say the plot's soiled? We'll see about that.

Mrs. Biocide: So many gallons of tears. What sewage? Frightful vertigo. I must find a sympathetic alias. Maybe the lion tamer can help.

Mr. Insecticide: What dominoes shall plague these criminal sentiments? Wait, just let me take a goddamn nap.

Mrs. Pesticide: Algorithms are the least of our concerns. Someone break out an almanac. Full moon, yes?

*

Scene: A coffeehouse. Various paintings on the walls. Gewgaws here and there. Each character sitting at a different table. Each character wearing pretty much the same garb. All characters are speaking at the same time. Each character will repeat his or her comment four times, using whatever tone, inflection, pace, etc. seems right. Tones can change with each repetition of the comment or stay the same. No one is really speaking directly to anyone else, though characters can occasionally glance at each other or make fleeting eye contact. The feeling is definitely not communal, but not isolationist either.

Mr. Viricide: Marital infidelity? Fat chance! Thirty-seven years of marriage and even my hemorrhoids remind me of my wife. We play "who hid the Preparation H?" I let her win.

Ms. Rodenticide: Sometimes the iron rod stabbing its way through my spine is simply my conscience. Other times it's a dowser. Yesterday I couldn't use the bathroom. Oh, need I continue?

Mr. Algicide: I guess it's my dream to set up a radio terminal in a fast-food playground. People have always called me ambitious, but I like to think I'm simply inspired. I'm in the headlines all the time; well, I should be.

Ms. Avicide: I get tired, very tired, in fact exhausted, when I think that the only funny thing in the world is that silly show, *Intercourse the Penguin*. I seldom survive a rerun without peeing in my pants.

Mrs. Biocide: Smoke, smoke, smoke. Everything burning, giving off smoke. Inner and outer. Essence and form. You know, in an alternate life I lecture about all this in Sanskrit. You ought to tune in sometime.

Mrs. Microbicide: For the love of God, would someone please just pass me the pepper.

Mr. Germicide: I've had it with crowbars. Force is not the solution!

Mrs. Bactericide: For sinus problems, I tear out a page of Aristotle's *Nicomachean Ethics* and mix it with a saline solution in a glass of warm water. Then I snort. Those driblets are my little phlegmy pedagogical pets. Who needs those damn cats!

Mr. Insecticide: I sing lullabies to the dead stars. I collect arrowheads from the old battlegrounds. I'm somewhat of a string nut. All kinds of strings, literal and symbolic, I don't care. I don't distinguish anything from anything else anymore.

Ms. Herbicide: My friends call me Herbie; that is, well, my one friend calls me Herbie. We're in love. It's everlasting. I'm stocking up on tinfoil.

Mr. Molluscicide: I'll never forget having to read *Ivanhoe* to the entire school body when I was ten. Ever since, I've despised missionaries. And plumbers. And I don't care for my feet. I think my knees are classic, but my ankles—does anyone have the refund number?

Ms. Parasiticide: Nine times out of ten, my moniker is "Kiss Me Sebaceous." I don't give a rat's ass what you think. I've got my reasons. The tenth time, I go by "Laundry Jell-O."

Mrs. Pesticide: I'm a sucker for comic-book humor. Oh, did someone set the alarm?

Mr. Acaricide: Gerald! Gerald! Hey, Gerald! Where the hell are you? Geralllllllld!!!

Mr. Fungicide: Semaphore is to signal what sofa is to couch. Now listen closely, my comrades, the ceiling is falling. Bring your toupees. We will practice wearing them like the futuristic monocles of a master race of Nurbs.

Mr. Nematocide: I've decided to move all my pet projects inside. What do you mean, heat? I have to defend myself sometimes, don't I? Oh juicy day, where is your juice?

*

from Jay Jordan's "A Review of The Southside Company's
Production of B. Henrico Boston's 'Endless' Play'"
(published in *The Topeka Sundial*; June 15, 2006)

"…while this production features many accessible elements, including generous infusions of universal humor, "The Endless Play" is probably not for those who demand that their *t*s be crossed and their *i*s dotted. There is an abundance of ambiguity and obliquity here and much circuitousness when it comes to narrative. Also, most of the interactions between characters do not unfold in a typically conversational fashion; in fact, in many sections of the play, several (unrelated) dialogues occur simultaneously, the various conversational threads blending and conflicting, making singular listening difficult, if not impossible. One such example, occurring about an hour into the staging, involves four different sets, each separated by partitions along the front of the stage. In the first area, there is a conversation occurring between a businessman and a car mechanic. They are engaged in a matter-of-fact debate over whether the businessman should be able to swap a lamb he himself raised on his family farm and recently slaughtered for "four über-safe tires." In the second area, set in a doctor's examination room, a nurse is trying to convince a man to accept an injection which has a 67% chance of "transferring upon him irrevocable immortality," but which also has a 33% chance of causing immediate death. In the third area, a tutor is addressing four students, giving them a history lesson. We clearly understand that the tutor is fabricating dates and events; the students, however, are utterly enraptured. In the fourth area, a man is playing chess seemingly against himself, arguing (with himself) as to whether various moves are or are not against the rules. Finally, when he is checkmated (by himself), he aggressively sweeps all the chess pieces onto the floor but immediately reassembles the board and begins the game anew.

As a playwright, Boston works ambitiously to develop particular themes and commentaries regarding history and the individual's relationship to society. And, while the particular characters and situations of the play are engaging in themselves, they often strike one as being strangely superfluous, oddly replaceable, even unmemorable. It is as if Boston randomly drew the ideas for these characters and their related plots from a hat, when he could have just as easily picked other characters and other situations. In the end, there is nothing particularly distinct about any of these characters or their monologues or dialogues. And yet, they are somehow compelling, perhaps *because of* their banality and the unsettling implication that they are being offered as reflections of our own lives. Director Shelley Goldworth does a good job of furthering Boston's dry explorations of such issues as the ongoing homogenization of America at the hands of capitalism and the ultimate indistinguishability of one (American) life from another. Sustaining audience engagement while also hinting that their engagement is ultimately unwarranted is a particularly difficult balance to invoke, but Goldworth and her actors—especially Jill Kessler as Ms. Avicide and Michael Dolter as Mr. Molluscicide—do a commendable job, careful not to collapse into either sentimental realism or overly detached meta-surrealism.

Two of the more interesting junctures in the play occur at "intermission" and at the "end" of the production. After Mrs. Parasiticide (adeptly played by Tess Hammersmith) realizes that she is actually a transgendered man and that what she had thought were multiple orgasms were actually "homunculus cramps," the (bright) lights come up. Ushers march down the aisles, urging the audience to move towards the lobby, if so inclined. It is clearly intermission; however, on-stage a volatile argument suddenly erupts between Mrs. Bactericide (awkwardly but sympathetically played by Hillary Munderstun) and Mr. Viricide (for the most part clumsily played by Austin Tucker) over whether Horatio Clement (a 14th Century English poet) would have made a better Prime Minister than Winston Churchill. The audience is unsure what to do. Isn't this intermission? Then why is there still activity on-stage? What is the protocol in such a situation? The content of the dialogue is overtly absurd and inspires restrained laughter from the audience. And yet the anxiety of unknowing (regarding whether to leave or sit back down) is collectively palpable.

Similarly, at the "end" of the play, when each of the characters realizes that he or she is simply a character in a play and not a real person, and each actor realizes that he or she is not operating autonomously but rather following the dictates of a script, and the members of the audience are barraged with the suggestion that they are not real people whose lives are authentically and spontaneously unfolding, but rather, at least at the moment at hand, subjects in a paradigmatic context operating according to conditioned expectations and assumptions, the (even brighter than at intermission) lights come up again. The play, as a theatrical event with a *de facto* beginning, middle, and end, is clearly over (there is, however, no curtain call, just an abrupt silence and vacating of the stage). However, two or three minutes later, just as the audience is moving confidently towards the exit, Mr. Nematocide (proficiently played by Gerald DeLimne) stamps (back) onto the stage and barks epithets at Mr. Acaricide (a bit dryly played by Eric Vosso), who a few seconds later appears from stage-left in a wheelchair, speeding across and propelling himself from the stage, crashing onto the floor below in a pile of metal and limbs. Looking around, I noticed that the remaining audience members (again) seemed unsure as to how they should proceed. They were captured utterly in limbo, somehow no longer official audience members but also not fully reintegrated into one or another aspect of their ("non-theatrical") everyday lives. Finally, after fifteen or so minutes, everyone had left but me. It was clear that the "endless" dialogue would not cease until I too left, which I did after a few more minutes.

The play under Goldworth's direction serves to illustrate Boston's preoccupation with the seamlessness with which humans shift and segue from role to role and the discomfort we experience when that fluidity is in any way hampered. Also well illustrated is the way in which our reactive egos so often run the show despite the fact that we collectively pride ourselves on being informed, progressive, and even enlightened people. Occasionally Boston's absurdist leanings, under Goldworth's direction, eclipse the very serious messages of the play, resulting in moments of slapstick comedy or even outright buffoonery, but all in all this is a very effective production of a particularly difficult play. 87/100.

*

Internet Visual Style Guide
Sixteen Types of Poison in Search of an Author
a website design project estimate from webmistress Adele Fortinbras
www.xmirafortinbras.com

I. Images as chiaroscuro for poison pellets and word-
   bombs a. Size (Proximal)
      i. If horizontal: width=127 pixels
      ii. If vertical: height=147
   b. Location/Properties (Sheol, Southside Company)
      i. Alignment=Left
      ii. Spacing
         1. Horizontal= 5
         2. Vertical= 5
II. Text for mixed-use audience apposition and fourth wall penetration
   a. Acts/Scenes/Sub-Scenes/Appendices/
      i. Font color= #002b73
      ii. Font face= arial, helvetica, sans-serif
      iii. Size= 2
      iv. Style= Bold
      v. HTML tag= <font color="#002b73" face="arial, helvetica, sans-serif"
size="2">stage directions, lighting, intonation, accent, wardrobe</font>
   b. Dialogic/Monologic Content
      i. Font color= #002b73
      ii. Font face= arial, helvetica, sans-serif
      iii. Size= 2
      iv. Style= normal
      v. HTML tag = <font color="#002b73" face="Arial, helvetica, sans-serif" size="2">
III. Example of HTML code "Mr. Algicide: "All around me, detritus—but I'm clean, clean, squeaky
clean."
<img alt="" src="https://www. B.henricoboston.com/accounttempfiles/account400615/images/file-
name.gif" longdesc="" align="left" border="0" height="134" hspace="5" vspace="5" width="147" />
<font color="#002b73" face="Arial, helvetica, sans-serif" size="2">poison, sixteen,
author

</font>
<palign="left"><font color="#002b73" face="Arial, helvetica, sans-serif" size="2"> Ms. Rodenticide: "I
can't commit to things that vacillate. Find someone else." e

<a href="http://www.cci.org/site/link critic here/" target="_blank">description of actor(s), roles, critical
attention, Boston's vitae</a>

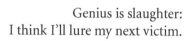

Genius is slaughter:
I think I'll lure my next victim.

III.

At this point, I think someone should intervene
       and reevaluate the data,
       fill in the subjects
       as to the true nature of this experiment.

I'm tempted to offer myself complete immunity:
       please see me as I want to be seen.

I know, it's unpardonable for me to have developed
       so strong a resistance to this lexical venom:
it's as if my life is a digital dream
       superimposed upon collective scar tissue
       thousands of years old.

The highway is a bite mark on my adopted sister's thigh.
All these singers with their songs about *the road, the road.*
You're not giddy, Louisa, you're as mercurial as a menopausal diva snooping around a sweatshop. When
does your tea party resume, anyway?
Early November, and the clouds still remind me of a New Jersey nursing home.
Hear hear, in the name of what might grow like wild grass in our future guts.
I'll agree that I've wandered from the heart of things.
I need a primer. And a preface. And an epilogue. I can handle the rest.
That's *Mr.* Circle to you.
Don't you think some messiah is bound to come along soon and reboot our feelings?

I continue to bore myself, always bemoaning the effects of time. You'd think I was Dorian Gray. In fact,
does anyone have a mannequin that could pass as my double?
"I do," interrupted Antonin Artaud Jones, the son of actors Gwen Hope Michelet and Drew Hampton Jones.

"It comes installed with thumbs, lubricated orifices, amygdalae, blinking eyes, and body hair that grows in the dark."

Hmm. Whatever. Let me ask you this: do you find that you're less and less interested in circumstances?

You mean, how do I reconcile my B-attitude with my somewhat Zen outlook?

"Simple," Antonin again interrupted, "I practice levitation, holding Matsuo Basho's *Zoku Sarumino*. Once in flight, and holding for at least three minutes, I tear a few pages from the book and study them as they eventually drift downwards."

I like to watch boiling water until it cools to room temperature. Then I like to reheat it, begin the process again. Once I did this over and over for eight days straight without eating or talking on the telephone. I like to stare at myself in the mirror without blinking until I tear and see myself in triplicate, encased in an iridescent aura, hundreds of miniature carnies performing somersaults and laughing. Sounds interesting, but I've got a mob here right now, so it might be a little difficult for me to set up a credible communion. Come to think of it, I could really use one of those mail-order wizards. Out of luck. It's Sunday, and it's been 11:56am for three hours. Well, let's keep our eyes on the thought of sunset. Let that be the jazz towing us out of this ditch.

Something nags at me like the hum of a leaf blower,
a dis-ease I can't quantify with a measuring cup.

I visited the famous New Orleans tailor, Mr. Blane LeManc,
hired him to fashion a polyester suit of grief
in honor of my floating friends
(I will only wear it
on overcast mornings, fifth Mondays, perhaps Easter).

PS. Despite much training in hypnosis, neurolinguistic programming, and traditional legerdemain, I still blanch under the auspices of The Tempestuous Woman.

*

Photo of Adele "Xmira" Fortinbras, known as
"Mistress Xmira," two days after the suicide of
her devoted submissive, B. Henrico Boston
(Marcus, SD: February 16, 2009)

IV.

Rene Lamaude, possessed by a perfunctory
    commitment to neo-futurism with its narco-digital
        intoxicants, delivered his organs to the agent.
Droid threw his dice into the fountain
    and proceeded to feed the pigeons
        his only remaining
            dictum.

          Dawn, a desiccant extraordinaire but overly temperate,
                yellow as Abraham's inner chicken,
           dispatched Death to tap me on the shoulder
            ("The trick," some rolfer offers, "is to never
        give up on The Laboratory at the Edge of the World."
           But what a flagrantly xenophobic joke!).

Mr. Lamaude's zaplet was a pommel—"This is what I
    mean," said Droid, "amid the poesis rises
        again your rude non sequitur, irreal assault
    on logic. I say skin all posers and liquify
their pockmarked flesh."—pommel pronounced *p(u)mmel*
    (histrionic Droid clutching his chest
        as Lamaude, flaunting pantaloons
and a tricorne, drools over a 1770
        Chippendale Rorschach).

I *do* actually know six Luddites who attended that debutante party.
Let me guess: now they speak in circles about the transcendence of constructs?
Well, it's a tradition, you know, *raison d'être*, talent show, parade, wormwood extravaganza with totems of absinthe and chocolate Listerine.
That's fine, but I know we *will* claim the celestial. I'll eventually shed this tired self in a mall parking lot, bury it amongst the bones of rodents and the repetitive mumblings of this or that bowlegged clerk.
You go on and on, don't you? You sure are impressed with the opinions of all these Does and Joneses and Blacks.
I admit it, I'm hoping they'll turn in positive reports, help me seal the deal with that redhead who always gives me music when I bog down in the doldrums.

Mr. Lamaude nails Droid to a decree
        one evening along the Styx
          simulacrum littered with dinghies and broods.
When all else fails, he dons an ox head
and spins like a dervish into a razor sleep:

two deep pockets and a swarm of wasps.
"Say *nihil obstat, mon cher perdant*," he mutters
  to a naked man demonstrating asanas on a diving board,
thousands of bowler hats drifting from a piebald sky.
  You've always said, haven't you,
  that there's only one resolute, pure atomic fact?

  All spokes lead to overdrawn bank accounts and the debacle of a suspicious growth.
  Are you accustomed to starting over and wearing nothing in the face of an audit?
  Let me respond this way: I'd rather leave footprints on the water,
  my life like a rainbow doming Clytemnestra's million-dollar courtyard.
  Subpoint B: do pear cores rot redemptively on your windowsills?
  I'm unwilling to go on record as saying anything more than
  what I really want is to get these engines turning.

"Such is a meticulous sartori," shouts Mr. Lamaude,
  "pits filled with clichés and fiery beasts—iron
    balls catapulted from a makeshift mouth
    screwed into a dead, plucked body
      bloody on a spit." He furrows his brow,
      puckers his lips, and inflates his chest.
"Go ahead, buddy, foam at the bit," Droid peremptorily replies,
  "your tripe is, I admit, lambent. You are forever
wowing deadpan logicians with your cheap fireworks:
    hollow, bucolic, swiveling, maneuvering
    your well-oiled torso beyond the usual hyperbole
      towards an isolated, muddy absolute."
Lamaude and Droid, hand in hand at the guillotine.

  Slag—
  no one sparing anyone slack—tracking
  through casinos and churchyards unto a mortgage payment,
  one more divestment in drag with encomiums,
  purified for the coming of a consummate thespian-messiah.

AMERICA,

oh mistress,

I have forgotten my safe word!
I have forgotten my safe word!
I have forgotten my safe word!
I have forgotten my safe word!

(Velvet gloves are used during any activity that involves penetration. All enemas, catheters, razors, and needles are used once and disposed of appropriately. All inserted instruments are sheathed with Manger (midsized) condoms and, following usage, soaked in a bleach solution in addition to a high-powered and consumer-mandated antibacterial. Dildos are boiled for exactly two minutes and thirteen seconds and subsequently soaked in a bleach solution. Bandages and ropes are machine-laundered in a SMA-endorsed launderette by SMA-trained practitioners. All equipment surfaces are scoured prior to staging with a mixture of alcohol and water heated to a minimum of two hundred degrees Fahrenheit.)

V.

All night the mad camellias ogle
    through a cold, fogged window
as I dream of factories, assembly lines, a new theater of cruelty.

Let's bandage this dénouement—you or me?
How about each of us exposing a cicatrix   (sic(k) of tricks)
to our audience—we, their inpatients, clutching our fetish objects.

Get ready, Mr. McCalister, biologists in the cathedral,   (cat(he) dra(w)ls)
the shoppers conversing in a language
you've never heard before.

"*Meambular curvotsic sigly*," said Cormal Xyium   (more like corporal, no?)
    to Lypad Flooqy. "The stage
        is phylogenetic. They have their instruments."

There's a confession I'd like to make,
    but this lifeblood keeps flowing
        in a different direction.   (is the mic plugged in?)

I must admit that when shove comes to push   *(pusato shivea, linga)*
and push itself comes to a point; when my life   *(relata ante vis agonia)*
is reduced to an index finger, I concede, emphatically, scratch.   *(reducta vio anteunio)*

Q. Many critics consider your early work to be Diluvian in nature. You have certainly moved in a different direction stylistically, at least with this new book. Do you think you will ever return to your earlier style or have you moved on for good?
A. I can't say what will happen in the future. Anything's possible, obviously. I do think, though, that many of America's best poems were crafted by the so-called Diluvian Poets—first, second, and third generations—a number of whom were my teachers or at least muses. No one, in my opinion, can shake a reader like a skilled Diluvian.
(interview with Saul Bradshaw, winner of the 1998 James Height Poetry Award)

I'm overwhelmed by a diluvian sense
that if it weren't for my nubile days on a Parisian quay,
wind light with a light brown rain and a sense sublime
of Romanticism, I'd throw myself off the Golden Gate Bridge.

I recall that a diluvian shadow on Louisa's face reminded me
of November in Rhode Island, the bistro beside the Providence,

that carnie with hair as red as a Radio Flyer.

"Now they want a memoir? Goddamn alphabetic vultures. This is not Diluvian, never has been. I am no less than a trans-categorical, subaquatic bomb erupting the academy's secret narrative."
(comment made by Saul Bradshaw at his 2006 competency hearing)

Beneath this gray umbrella of diluvian doubt,
stumbling from awning to awning,
I go to meet my mercurial date,
Memory—she shall deliver
such delicious strokes of leather!

Q. Are you implying a suicide?
A. I'm implying that if it weren't for a modicum of poesis made manifest through the verses of a Beauriad or the canvases of a Linlapoire, I'd release my death grip and spiral into Guganania's black hole. How dreary is a life bereft of antiquity, a life whose metonymies once bestowed upon a reader divine allegories of the Bestiary. I have been reduced to digits and styrofoam—this is why I confess and dream.
Q. Do you imply that you are in essence the fourth draft of The Cosmic Masterpiece? Wait, wait, I don't mean some manifestation of metaphor, some ratiocination of a star in nova, I mean the singular and inseparable manifesto of the universe itself! And please, please, don't avoid the issue through flattery. The best of the best have called me the Prime Transubstantiation itself, and it hasn't gotten them off the hook.
A. I leave my canonic posterity in the hands of The Cosmic Editor—equipped with three brains, twelve eyes, and twenty-four computer screens from which redaction becomes holy writ.
(mock interview between Saul Bradshaw and painter Devon Humboldt, both of whom were patients at the Morganton Psychiatric Unit from 2006-2009, performed as part of a "rehabilitative play" in April 2008)

QueenE Monochromatix: Are you trying to seduce me with sugar and the remnants of love letters I once read while covered in dirt up to my lips?
QueenE Moddled: Uh, I'm in a junkyard filled with empty tin cans, beer cans to be exact. I haven't had a slice of brie in so many years that my olfactory senses have turned to cardboard. And I'm supposed to play your educated jester? And not even have a croquet mallet to my name? Forget it, find another gopher for this cheap synthetic advertisement.

…out of the velvet darkness, armed with a bare bodkin, a coonskin hat perched above iron helmet and pearl earrings, arrives Sir Flunky, last of the knighted gentry. "Yo dawg, where de cat at?" he bellows. Then a thousand-pound iron ball catapulted from the forest fells the poor bastard. A small crowd comprised of ladies-in-waiting and vestal virgins gives him a standing ovation.

Jeannie appears, wig in hand. She has been shaving her pubic hair daily for six months and can't wait to grind her stubble on Sir Desmond's plump and pasty visage. "Come and get it," she whispers into the telephone. And Sir Desmond somehow manages to jab his right pinky into an electric socket.

"There's nothing like the smell of sardines on a hot and humid day when you're a fishmonger with literary aspirations," said the sad old man who witnessed the suicide of Sir Desmond. "Just wait until I catch my sardines by electric socket. All the hospitals and Carcinogen Societies will be giving me their book awards."

Q. So what's next for you?
A. Uh…nothing. Finally there is no next.
Q. Do you think you'll return to a Diluvian style?
A. What's a Diluvian style?
(interview with Saul Bradshaw, following his 2009 release from the Morganton Psychiatric Unit)

Sir Flunky drowns in a pickle vat,
      his last syllables swallowed by brine,
his ribald stories jarred for the true America!

You know, I think I've lost my father's ashes.
The future has been reduced to a mere conspiracy.
I've hired a digital cartographer to remap my vision,
someone who can juggle while drawing boundaries—
with one hand, a fire hydrant; the other, a bonobo.
I get so tired I can't even sketch the end;
therefore, I call upon Manut to bring a pencil.
At some point, something caves in. Then, it's downhill,
the protagonists rehearsing all night, keeping the oracles awake.
"Manut," I ask, "have you sketched the myriad shapes?"
His silence reminds me of a yawning chimney.
Do we now scoff at complacencies and shift our tonal grids?
Well, the hanging committee did offer a reasonable explanation.
I think there's a hole, actually, where there shouldn't be one,
and I've just jumped into it, clutching my letter opener.
I suppose a *deus ex machina* is out of the question?
It's that or a *pas de deux*—*s* or *x*?
This kind of pressure tends to bring out the juggernaut in me.

SECTION FIVE

...entrance without fanfare...much fluttering...exit without fanfare...

I.

Sometimes by dawn JD smolder blue, strum his red guitar as sunrise
drape over the house. He skim headlines, the sports section, the obits
over fruit and toast. He consider a sick day, sick with success and failure.
But onward! a day in the gullet of his cul de sac, the intestine of the mall.
JD sell ten new stereos! Then dusk arrive, beating moths and deep sighs.
Dame Melancholy wink; JD's swagger wane, so predictable. He muster,
'gain pound the 'ol dinner table, lament his days 'nother sundown by.

II.

When JD a child, fail to thrive, the Hippocrates prescribe him a three-
dimensional beta blocker, a corticosteroid delivered via a karmic patch.
They lavish him with milk chocolate after he endorse they diagnostics.
"Oh mama of resilience," they incant, "virgin of immunity, sanctify this
regimen scrip for scrip. But no worry, JD, you're healthy as a trapezist."
JD remember Nurse Gisela read to him from *Revelation*; when offended,
she apoplex in German. Forward back forward, JD faltering convalesce.

III.

JD drag along for hours his backbone. When he lag hazy, he tongue-
grind until he palate blood. That rev him right up. JD inappropriate
with shoppers, tell a repeat customer she "*la soeur laide de Medusa.*"
He scrawl with blue marker on a display case: "Misunderstood again."
A colleague cringe in ye stockroom. Someone report him to Mr. Grrr.
Mr. Grrr write JD a warning. JD envision Mr. Grrr in ye electric chair,
torque him twitch twitch. Ah, bemoan JD, I a man of such wasted wit.

IV.

A Saturday alone, all things possible, a love of fate and a love of awe.
JD straddle a stool, do a romance spread, he and his eyes cross-armed
in these fluxing foretells rise pass rise. The Widewe card: unto danger.
Conflict and concord betweox The Jester and The Goldwine. JD shuffle,
draw The Nine Gærstapan: surrender prior to famine shall protect him.
He conclude with The Opposer card, will rightly foot-drag in transition,
then flush on, a true shuck-and-jive Trickster—but so by God bona fide.

V.

Speeding through denial 'burbs to a center-city pain-point
with its strobing light and shrieking, crimson siren, JD now
concede: he a charlatan, a Pierrot trapped in a pantomime,
tossing he black skullcap into an audience of columbines.
He imagination is corrupt, calumnious. JD indulge heself
with self-applause, clap 'til he hands bleed. He wipe bloody
palms on he cheeks and smirk. JD repeat this until he bored.

VI.

JD a true auteur of lucid dreaming. He suspend physics, materialize
new lapis worlds. He choreograph cold stars, repressed impulses he
north star now. JD plant flags in ye protean soil of his subconscious.
He transcend memory, forsake his name in ye darkness e'er unfurling.
He have no need for cue cards, trash his sales pitch, miss departmental
powwows. Betimes JD lotus at ye dry edge of a word-tide counting
cumulus-birds. From ye fatigue to ye frisson, his oh so ephemeral be!

VII.

Mantra after mantra, waiting: JD embody a pseudo-mystique of
canonical patience, playing web-scrabble with two indigo children.
JD pay a bill, send a modest donation to an animal rights organization.
Life ahoy, but here with a wife ebullient. No negations, but rather
paradoxes. JD am not transcendently prone, but think of himself as
cool chameleon, reincarnated seeking sadhu, jockish in his tank top.
JD hum, no complaint, bubble soak for hours in a middle-class bath.

VIII.

Under the balmy auspices of honeysuckle sedatives, JD pray again,
the sky cloudy with spacecraft fume and some tyrant's head-smoke.
A dead finch lie beneath the rhododendron. JD want: a commission.
Instead he get six disgruntled customers and a critique from Mr. Grrr.
JD reject notions of consequence; he say, "causality a dated religion."
He wax resilient, amuse himself with limericks, taunts, non sequiturs.
He give a man in a kilt with a red mohawk an unauthorized discount.

IX.

JD tan in a magnolia park, look at photos of his
first cousin eternally removed by a collapsing sun,
a neurological diagnosis glued to the album page.
JD tremble under a blue sky, wonder if he too host
the genetic worm insatiable, gnawing through his own
cursed loam: destined for madness, a dark descent.
Sometimes JD feel the worm teeth chomp chomp.

X.

JD's saunter from the breakroom to the parking lot be a spectacular
spin-out. He cologne in fungal musk, put on a lupine face. He throb
in his newfound release like a traitor spitting in The Dark Queen's
vichyssoise. He key Mr. Grrr's car, squat and shit under an oak tree.
JD snarl several rhymes into his handheld recording device, dash his
handheld mirror to the littered asphalt, behold his total disassemblage.
Here, then, is JD's bottom, who he be shatter into a thousand pieces.

XI.

"The theoretical," JD say, "is for the caged and collared lapdog."
He add, "I'm about the nipple, Eros, ash; the rest just incidental."
JD frequently a crazy Buddha—push not, pull not. He a black hole
and new sun rolled into one. He pee his initials in the fresh snow.
"Bring my 1895 Tula," he blurt, waxing thespian, "the doubters
'round the knolls, and I do taste murder on my lips." JD conclude:
"No shame thusly to confess, the biblical killer doth reside in me."

XII.

JD wake on Sunday morning, his mouth a long, serrated snout.
His right arm soon become a fin, his navel an anus. "Begorrah,"
he whimsical brogue, "to Mac Lir's watery depths 'm me bound."
JD fill his tub, practice his thrust, lift, and drag. "I shall indeed,"
he proclaim, "holystone me spinal cord into a purty lateral line."
JD's lungs turn to gills. He crave salt. Then, his famed departure.
JD swim oceans wooing marlin, eventually fall for a blue whale.

XIII.

JD am studying the nature of a pause. A small trapdoor open
in the infinity beyond his closed eyes, and JD catapult into light
as if ejecting from an airplane. His movements omnidirectional,
JD soar through green and violet landscapes, hear Canadian geese,
his boyhood priest incanting, someone tap percussive offbeat
on a manual typewriter. JD get this no pause, it *une fenêtre sainte*.
When JD come to, he weep in the long grass, beneath a willow.

XIV.

JD stutter in ye presence of Yahweh's dogs—slam doors, hunker
in his trenches. Ye dogs froth, froth like malfunctioning machines.
Once, in his days of grass and mud, JD know how to alpha them,
but now, gripped in ye suburban vortex, he pursued, tracked as he
stir his envy, reread Aquinas and Augustine, doze, deny, longing.
Monday dusk: JD in a corner, Yahweh's dog's growl snap growl.
In his Tuesday vision, JD am one of them—four-legged, in ye pack.

XV.

JD dream he have terminal cancer, Mr. Grrr with bullhorn mocking,
"How it feel to live, JD, in the shadow of the 'ol Reaper knocking?"
JD guffaw, riposte that he been waiting for some such circumstance
all his yeller days, a reason to surrender his breath as he know it, as he
heretofore map it, as if under this circumstance, end in sight, can he
now justify being free. JD wake, bug-eye, body ache. He say, "what
a bum break." He straitjacket-jacket. He handcuff-cuffs. He lariat-tie.

XVI.

Along shifting borders of envy, a valiant battle each day JD wage
against *das Ich*, which enticeth him with the pleasures of delusion.
JD picture Christ in the desert, the circle in the sand, angels finally
descending with rewards of ambrosia. JD meditate for three hours
motionless despite hunger pangs, back spasms, a fly on his philtrum.
"Salvation," he say, "is grace received through practiced dissolution."
JD release, grasp—J̶D̶, JD, J̶D̶, JD—this his bliss, this his perdition.

XVII.

JD dwell in the clutches of scarcity, haunted by abysmal sales,
ephemeral spikes, an economy prone to volatile mood swings.
This the pulse of his inner exile, JD feel endangered like a red-
bellied harvest mouse—top hat, wristwatch, corduroy trousers,
handwringing unto a paycheck. JD sink into eddies of doubt,
anxiety like a garrote, gorging on fattening foods and base TV:
failsafe methods distract him narcissist from his unfailing guilt.

XVIII.

JD ogle heself by sunrise, release a doom of he lacerated childhood
with its savage to puerile tibia, carpet-bombing of threats, imposed
regrets, unreadable psychiatric reports. JD renounce he ambivalence,
residue of old tapes, eschew he shackles, so as to chuck he long anger.
Despite insomnia, fever, pails of bloated frogs from God know where,
JD undo the stigma of he parents' misprisions: he now Albion, Uriel,
he n' longer the Candide who ma shatter he wrist in drug-addled rage.

XIX.

JD dash an impressionistic self-portrait, burn it on the winter solstice.
He shave his head and stash the clippings to tailor a new voodoo doll.
He vow to respond to questions with only violent laughter or outrage.
He dismiss all answers as incorrigible clichés, deconstruct divinations:
Kuai Tui Chi'en become *Chien Ching K'an*: chagrin surge through JD
like a swollen river. JD pox the mall, blow off thirteen customers, flip
his nametag in Mr. Grrr's eye—he bellow his glorious exit, "*Il est fini.*"

XX.

Boulders in ye umber field brood in ye heat. Even kudzu wince beneath
ye cane of August. JD sit, Zen Man of ye Suburbs, his mornings suffused
with neither hope nor dread, evenings hush with ye McMansion ennui.
JD clip roses and harvest cucumbers, fill blue birdbaths, wheel trashcans
to ye end of a street on Wednesdays. Slowly JD's diversions removed—
accomplishment, meaning, excess—remain an eternal moment, heartbeat,
pure space: ye ageless unfolding devoid of reference. Bless JD's details.

Acknowledgments

The authors thank the editors of the following journals, in which excerpts from this work first appeared, often in different form: *Cavalier Literary Couture*, *In Posse Review*, *New York Quarterly*, *Presa*, and *X-Peri*.

Credits and Source List for Images used in *The New Arcana*

PAGE	IMAGE	SOURCE
12	Image # 1647108	© tillsonberg/istock;
14 (top)	Image # 10144475	© Eyeidea®/istock
14 (bottom)	Detail/Michelangelo's Sistine Chapel (1508-12)	Public domain http://www.hayadan.org.il/does-evolution-disprove-god-0711/
17	"Cannibals" Gravure de Théodore de Bry (1562)	Public domain en.wikipedia.org/wiki/Image:Cannibals.23232.jpg
22	Image # 6072050	© Arpad Benedek/istock
23	Image # 516	© Bruce Livingstone/istock
24	Image # 10784377	© Yuriy Zelenenkyy/istock
26 (top)	Image # 9882140	© Tova Teitelbaum/istock
26 (bottom)	Image # 11548252	© Paolo Cipriani/istock
29 (left)	Image # 2275159	© erik thuro/istock
29 (right)	Image # 12877485	© Henrik Jonsson/istock
31	Image # 17096425	© Francesco Santalucia/istock
35	Image # 13551348	© Christopher Badzioch/istock
40 (top)	Image # 20855177	© Craig Dingle/istock
40 (bottom)	Image # 12667183	© Ivan Burmistrov/istock
46	Image # 5998884	© archives/istock
47	Image # 5908841	© Justin Voight/istock
48	Image # 6118067	© James Blinn/istock
49	Image # 10106334	© oleg filipchuk/istock
50	Image # 5014520	© Andreas Reh/istock
51	Image # 4130820	© Cliff Parnell/istock
53	Image # 16213028	© Rolf Fischer/istock
54	Image # 9458333	© Pavel Yazykov/istock
55 (top)	Image # 8554949	© zhang bo/istock
55 (bottom)	Image # 9959194	© LUNAMARINA/istock
56	Image # 5656472	© Sarah Palmer/istock
57	Image # 4303780	© Ekna Kouptsova-Vasic/istock
61	Image # 6821273	© tunart/istock
62	Image # 10022296	© elkor/istock
63	Image # 9743009	© Trista Weibell/istock
82	Image # 4651415	© Ekaterina Solovieva/istock
87	Image # 9653429	© ZekaG/istock
88	"The Atomicist," Digital Collage	© 2011 Daniel Y. Harris
94	"Salome" Titian (circa 1515)	Public domain http://en.wikipedia.org/wiki/Image:Tiziano_salome.jpg#imagelinks
95	Image # 510567	© Tina Lorien/istock
97	Image # 2808597	© Famke Backx/istock

About the Authors

John Amen has facilitated over ten thousand traditional, digital, etheric, SE (spacio-ekphrastic), and subatomic missives, many of which have been collected into both static and kinetic amalgams. His channelings have single-handedly revived at least fourteen dead languages and been broadcasted on both terrestrial and TT (trans-terrestrial) frequencies. His self-proliferating digi.tome, *Quark on X*, was featured in CLC's *The Antimatter Project* and won the 2009 Cryophilia Award. His 2010 "auto-deconstruction," staged in Oslo, was the subject of the award-winning telementary *Parting Walls*. In 2014 he will host the eleventh annual Festival of Sabotage to be held at Station L16 in the Pacific Trash Vortex.

Daniel Y. Harris is a posthuman, humuncular, and anthropoidal hybrid. He is the Founder and Chief Executive Officer of the genetic engineering company, METACULI. Prototypes of the Metaculi Beliti, a replacement human being with organic skin interface, positronic brain, and protean libido, will be featured at the 2013 Cyclops Expo in Reykjavík. He is the author of the first secreted novel, *Closet of Vellum Thongs*, winner of the 2011 Simony C. Reflux Prize. His weekly blog, *Pleonastic Gnat*, is a standard in the posthuman industry. On Sundays and Tuesdays, he rides a hand and foot trike though East Plumeria, speaking French to deciduous shrubs and the bevy of quail that has haunted him since 2002.